D1605567

People
Helping People

People
Helping People

by

Harold Ewing Burchett

MOODY PRESS
CHICAGO

Library of Congress Cataloging in Publication Data

Burchett, Harold Ewing.
    People Helping People.

    1. Peer counseling in the church. 2. Christian life—Baptist authors. I. Title.
BV4409.B87   248'.07   78-21546
ISBN 0-8024-6457-2

Printed in the United States of America

To the leaders of Quidnessett Baptist Church, who encouraged me to write this book.

Contents

Foreword

After Jesus had raised Lazarus from the dead, He instructed those who were nearby, "Take off the grave clothes and let him go" (John 11:44, NIV). How often those who have been instrumental in bringing eternal life to a soul have not been as faithful in releasing him from his binding "grave clothes" so that he might be free in the true, biblical sense (cf. John 8:32).

My earlier years as a Christian would have been much different if I had known then what the author of this book has shared with me. By the principles contained in this volume, God delivered me from the doubtings and binding habits that were destroying my marriage and that had completely incapacitated me for the ministry.

The author, Harold Burchett, pastor of a thriving, spiritual work at Quidnessett Baptist Church in southern Rhode Island, has been used by the Lord to encourage missionaries, pastors, Bible school students, and his own flock. Much contained in this book has been taught at various retreats and conferences, and in Columbia Bible College's special winter terms at Columbia, South Carolina.

Writing as one who has benefited from these basic Bible truths, I can verify that these practical, proved procedures are not mere theory of "nice ideas." On the contrary, the contents of this book, born out of a compassionate heart, have been refined in the crucible of personal experience and direct application to the lives of others.

Ephesians 4:15 states: "Grow up into him [Christ] in all things." Romans 8:29 indicates God's intention that we "be conformed to the image of his Son." By what process are we able to become more Christlike? What can produce greater effectiveness in our service for Christ? How can we help struggling ones with their spiritual difficulties? These questions and many others are answered in this book.

God-given gifts, knowledge, and experience qualify the author to write on this subject. However, the principles here considered are not for just a few specially talented people. Rather, they are written down so that any believer may discover what is true: God's Word, "quick and powerful," is capable of delivering from bondage and bringing an individual into mature effectiveness for Christ.

If you are seeking a new spirit in your ministry, a fresh way of approaching personal problems, a vital ministry in your church, something that will revolutionize your life and quicken your service for Christ—*This book is for you.*

RICHARD A. PETERS, Pastor
Grace Baptist Church
Cheshire, Connecticut

Preface

Hearing the lifeguard cough and choke brings little comfort to a drowning man.

In many quarters today the emphasis is on identifying with the friend in need—to sit where he sits. Weaknesses are bared and shared—often with little profit, or even with harm resulting.

Honesty is laudable, but what is most needed today is the ability to speak words that reach the troubled heart and fit the empty socket—words from God.

Despite these new currents of open-ended, frank sharing there is a large, unstirred sea of believers who remain mute in the presence of those needing their words of warning or encouragement. These Christians are virtual deadends for much of the truth received over the years. Under stress they might speak out and hurt, but so often they fail to reach out and heal.

I suppose every parent has experienced an awkward numbness in attempting to deal with his child in a time of crisis. Not only is it difficult to know what to say, but it is even more difficult to know how to say it.

Husbands and wives also might know an easing of tensions if only they had some skill in individual edification—that everyday type of counseling. Words need not be destructive. They can be very constructive.

The same is true in our churches. When members of a local assembly begin to edify and counsel one another effectively, new things take place. How different are these results from what is usually obtained through a group, or congregational, approach. This more personal, intensive sharing of life can be wonderful in its effects.

Scripture provides for both public and private ministries. Each is needed. This book deals with personal edification as an individual, private ministry. Building up another individual is a basic expression of one's own spiritual life.

In relating what I have personally learned in experience and practiced in my own service for Christ, I must make a confession. Much that is within these pages came very slowly and painfully to me over a period of many years. However, I know there is a "law of the harvest" that indicates that time required for learning lessons can be shortened when *"the righteous is a guide to his neighbor"* (Prov. 12:26, NASB).

Wide margins have been provided so that you may jot down personal notes of insight and application.

May God multiply His harvest by blessing this volume of personal counsel.

1

The Power
of a Wise Word
# of Counsel

"Death and life are in the power of the tongue" (Prov. 18:21, NASB).

The right word spoken at the right time can change a life. And we are continually involved in conversations with needy people.

REALIZE IT!

Imagine a tool so powerful that with it you can lift the level of another person's moral life, improve the quality of service for Christ, balance the wavering, lift the fallen, enlighten the ignorant, turn back the wayward, and much, much more! A good word of counsel is exactly that potent. By this I mean a deliberate, personal word to another for his upbuilding.

Here is a pertinent list of somewhat overlapping terms found in their various forms throughout our English Bible: *admonish, exhort, encourage, comfort, instruct, teach, counsel, warn, rebuke, reprove, direct, edify*.

Edifying conversation can have a marked effect on all basic areas of life. Speaking properly and prayerfully in the Spirit might affect a friend in such areas as (1) daily practices, (2) moods, (3) viewpoints or general outlook on life, (4) understanding truth, and (5) service for Christ.

In our daily involvement with other people, we touch on these facets of their lives more often than we perhaps realize. Personal encounters certainly are a vital part of life.

Uses of a Wise Word of Counsel

RESTORE PERSPECTIVE

Consider now with me various uses of a wise word of counsel.

Deep grief and even depression enter the lives of most good men. However, at times the real hurt comes from a loss of perspective. It is the responsibility of a Christian brother who is not in the choking smog to help.

Moods have handles. They can be turned about. When we lose our grip, a faithful word from a friend is often the very thing needed to put us back in control.

> The Lord God has given me the tongue of those who are taught, that I may know how to sustain with a word him that is weary (Isa. 50:4, RSV).

Marvelous it is that the tongue, so often an instrument of hurt, can actually sustain a weary friend.

> Anxiety in the heart of a man
> weighs it down,
> But a good word makes it glad
> (Prov. 12:25, NASB).

Notice carefully what it is that brings the transformation from the burdened heart to the relieved heart of gladness. It is nothing other than a good word. May God Himself equip you with good words as you work your way through this manual.

14

Mercy moves the rebel to the fork in the road. It is not kind to let him charge ahead in an unthinking manner. The willful man, daring God, may not be very attractive to a sensitive believer, but at least he deserves the opportunity for a showdown.

handwritten margin note: CHALLENGE THE REBEL LET NEVER ONE REBELLIOUS GO UNWARNED!!

You draw him to the fork in the road by a right use of God's authoritative Word.

For example, very carefully and deliberately read to a wayward friend the following words from the Bible:

> *My sheep hear my voice, and I know them, and they follow me* (John 10:27).

Next, say simply but earnestly, "Let us now read what the Shepherd says to you. If you are one of His sheep, you will hear this word from the Shepherd." At this point you would read a Scripture selected to bear on his particular sin pattern. It might be something like Galatians 5:19-21 or perhaps the following from Ephesians 5:3-7 (NIV):

handwritten margin note: ALSO, COULD USE PROV. 29:1 A MAN WHO HARDENS HIS NECK AFTER MUCH REPROOF WILL SUDDENLY BE BROKEN BEYOND REMEDY!

> *But among you there must not be even a hint of sexual immorality, or of any kind of impurity, or of greed, because these are improper for God's holy people. Nor should there be obscenity, foolish talk or coarse joking, which are out of place, but rather thanksgiving. For of this you can be sure: No immoral, impure, or greedy person—such a man is an idolater—has any inheritance in the kingdom of Christ and of God. Let no one deceive you with empty words, for because of such things God's wrath comes on those who are disobedient. Therefore do not be partners with them.*

While these words are still reverberating in the heart, ask pointedly, "Will you now obey what

God says to you? If so, I am willing to pray with you and help all I can." The word of admonition places the rebel at the fork in the road for his showdown.

UNDECEIVE THE MIND Truth frees one from sin. Some distortions will always be found in the thinking of those who continue in wrongdoing. Counsel opens truth in its proper dimensions before the mind.

It is a pity to give a blind person a better cane if instead you are able to help him see. Restoring spiritual sight will involve piercing through deceptions.

The apostle Paul predicts that in the last days, as things get worse, men will be found *"deceiving, and being deceived"* (2 Tim. 3:13).

> They do no know nor do they
> understand;
> They walk about in darkness
> (Psalm 82:5, NASB).

A man in a darkened room is not really helped by moving the furniture from his way. It is far better to turn on the light for him. This is done by a well-selected truth from Scripture, enforced by loving words of admonition.

> *The entrance of thy words giveth light; it giveth understanding unto the simple* (Psalm 119:130).

The word *entrance* here means "unfolding." The personal exhorter, then, aims at opening up truth that is lost to the deceived man. The heart must be reached. Scripture makes clear that the real issue is what a man says in his heart.

∴ MENTAL BELIEF IS NOT THE ISSUE, BUT WHAT'S DEEP INSIDE

16

*The fool hath said in his heart, There is no God.
They are corrupt, they have done abominable works,
there is none that doeth good* (Psalm 14:1).

Now compare this with Psalm 15:2: *"He that
walketh uprightly, and worketh righteousness, and
speaketh the truth in his heart."*

Often a quiet reminder of the simplest truth
has an explosive effect in the life of a deceived
and compromised Christian. For example, he
probably will have forgotten the very obvious
teaching of Proverbs 28:9: *"He that turneth away
his ear from hearing the law, even his prayer shall be
abomination."* It stabs home to the heart when
you say to him, "My friend, you cannot continue
both to disobey and to pray."

1 HINDRANCE TO PRAYER

No doubt, one of the most common misconceptions is that which enables a man to trifle
with the grace of God. Jude 4 mentions those
who are found *"turning the grace of our God into
lasciviousness"* even within the circle of believers.

The apostle Paul had the same thing in mind
in Galatians 5:13:

> For, brethren, ye have been called unto liberty; only
> use not liberty for an occasion to the flesh, but by love
> serve one another.

Therefore, if you see a fellow Christian striving to keep his confidence in Christ and at the
same time walking a contrary way, chances are
he is trying to calm his troubled conscience by
false notions. A key issue in his confusion will be
a distorted view of grace.

He will reason, "I was saved by grace, not by
works, and grace will get me through even
though things in my life are not right." He needs

to hear some fundamental truths such as the following stated simply and clearly: Grace does not make a way for us to keep our sins. Grace makes a way to stop sins. God's strength never energizes a rebel in the wrong. He is without life-flow from God even as a trolley car off the track is left without power.

Grace does not relieve the conscience so one can sin with less burden of heart. A sinning Christian is a contradiction in terms. The Holy Spirit being thus grieved will remove comfort and assurance from such a man.

Indeed, the free mercy of God trains us to say no to our wrong desires.

> *For the grace of God that brings salvation has appeared to all men. It teaches us to say "No" to ungodliness and worldly passions, and to live self-controlled, upright and godly lives in this present age, while we wait for the blessed hope—the glorious appearing of our great God and Savior, Jesus Christ, who gave himself for us to redeem us from all wickedness and to purify for himself a people that are his very own, eager to do what is good* (Titus 2:11-14, NIV).

HELP BREAK THE BONDS OF HABITUAL SIN

This critical matter will be handled in my discussion of what I call the *deliverance encounter*, covered in chapter 4. Some habits are so tenacious and enslaving that they require this more intense, dynamic approach. However, let me remind here of our Savior's good word in John 8:32:

> *And ye shall know the truth, and the truth shall make you free.*

18

Appropriate Scripture truth, reinforced by enlightening counsel and earnest prayer, can reach to the deep root of the trouble. Individual exhortation is a biblical, spiritual ministry. Therefore supernatural blessing accompanies it.

(For the weapons of our warfare are not carnal, but mighty through God to the pulling down of strong holds;) Casting down imaginations, and every high thing that exalteth itself against the knowledge of God, and bringing into capitivity every thought to the obedience of Christ (2 Cor. 10:4-5).

A soft answer turneth away wrath: but grievous words stir up anger.
The tongue of the wise useth knowledge aright: but the mouth of fools poureth out foolishness.
The eyes of the Lord are in every place, beholding the evil and the good (Prov. 15:1-3).

BREAK UP THE ARGUMENT CYCLE

The quiet, good word is powerful to put out the fires of anger whether they are raging against us or against someone else. *"And a soft tongue breaketh the bone"* (Prov. 25:15).

A certain cycle effect accompanies angry words. If one attacks another in anger, then the attacked person grows angry. This makes the attacker still more angry, and so on. *"A hot-tempered man stirs up strife"* (Prov. 15:18, NASB).

WHAT MARTI HAS EXPERIENCED ! --
ALSO SEE
PROV. 22:24,25

The man whose heart is bent on being personally edifying brings a solemn, eternal dimension into the heat of time and space. See this in Peter's familiar section. As a practical exercise, study the verses carefully, considering all the applications that come to mind.

Do not repay evil with evil or insult with insult,
but with blessing, because to this you were called so
that you may inherit a blessing.
For,
  Whoever would love life
  and see good days
  must keep his tongue from evil   JOHN!
  and his lips from deceitful speech.
He must turn from evil and do good;
he must seek peace and pursue it.
For the eyes of the Lord are on the righteous,
  and his ears are attentive to their prayer,
but the face of the Lord is against those
  who do evil.''

Who is going to harm you if you are eager to do
good? But even if you should suffer for what is right,
you are blessed. ''Do not fear what they fear; do not be
frightened.'' But in your hearts acknowledge Christ
as the holy Lord. Always be prepared to give an an-
swer to everyone who asks you to give the reason for
the hope that you have. But do this with gentleness
and respect, keeping a clear conscience, so that those
who speak maliciously against your good behavior in
Christ may be ashamed of their slander. It is better, if
it is God's will, to suffer for doing good than for doing
evil. For Christ died for your sins once for all, the
righteous for the unrighteous, to bring you to God.
He was put to death in the body but made alive by the
Spirit (1 Pet. 3:9-18, NIV).

OBJECTIONS   Many objections immediately come to mind
OVERRULED   when one considers taking up this ministry of
personal edification. Here are the general ones
in order:

1. ''No one should do such a thing; it is wrong
   to intrude yourself into the life of another.''

20

But it is never wrong to do right, and God says it is right that we have loving concern one for another—even to the extent of speaking seasonable words that apply to another's need. The whole matter of the honorable place of individual edification will be taken up in the following chapter.

2. "It is not my calling." While it is true that some have a particular gift and life calling to a more intense involvement in exhortation, all should commit themselves to it as occasion arises. Scripture makes abundantly clear that each Christian has this responsibility to some extent.

Accordingly, we are admonished:

> Let no unwholesome word proceed from your mouth, but only such a word as is good for edification according to the need of the moment, that it may give grace to those who hear (Eph. 4:29, NASB).

Furthermore we are warned against refusing to give the word of help to a brother in bondage.

> If thou forebear to deliver them that are drawn unto death, and those that are ready to be slain; if thou sayest, Behold, we knew it not; doth not he that pondereth the heart consider it? and shall not he render to every man according to his works? (Prov. 24:11-12).

3. Still a third objection is frequently heard against the idea of personal upbuilding: "It won't be received." Now it is to be understood that God nowhere urges us to take a mad dog by the ears. It is exceedingly un-

21

wise, Proverbs instructs us, to reprove a scornful fool. But seasonable, fitting words will often slip the defenses and get through to the heart. Learn to speak such words. It must be remembered that the art of admonition is never accomplished without love. Loving to "straighten people out" is not the same as loving those who are crooked in their ways. The counselor must be right in face, in voice, in manner, and, above all, in heart if he is to be an effective instrument of God. Bluntness and tactlessness are not the marks of spiritual courage. But one must not be overly sparing, either.

THIS IS PERHAPS MY CENTRAL NEED OF IMPROVEMENT!

> *Faithful are the wounds of a friend; but the kisses of an enemy are deceitful* (Prov. 27:6).
> *There is that speaketh like the piercings of a sword: but the tongue of the wise is health* (Prov. 12:18).

Finally, one who lives in a wrong way will not speak a right word. It must be the sincere heart itself that gives forth a telling word of exhortation to another life.

> *Out of the same mouth proceedeth blessing and cursing. My brethren, these things ought not so to be. Doth a fountain send forth at the same place sweet water and bitter? Can the fig tree, my brethren, bear olive berries? either a vine, figs? so can no fountain both yield salt water and fresh. Who is a wise man and endued with knowledge among you? let him shew out of a good conversation his works with meekness of wisdom. But if ye have bitter envying and strife in your hearts, glory not, and lie not against the truth. This wisdom descendeth not from above, but is earthly, sensual,*

22

devilish. For where envying and strife is, there is confusion and every evil work. But the wisdom that is from above is first pure, then peaceable, gentle, and easy to be intreated, full of mercy and good fruits, without partiality, and without hypocrisy. And the fruit of righteousness is sown in peace of them that make peace. (James 3:10-18).

4. "I can't! I simply am not equipped." This final objection rises in the hearts of all at one time or another. The remainder of this book is aimed at helping here.

2

Personal Counsel in God's Scheme of Things

A good word spoken in the Spirit brings new life.

Now let us consider how this plan of one individual speaking personally to another for the serious purpose of edifying fits into God's scheme of things. Especially, we will see how individual encouragement and teaching belong in the life of a local church fellowship.

Both public ministry and the various forms of private, individual edification are needed in any living church.

God's Word furthermore indicates two manners in which each type of ministry is to be performed, namely, spontaneous and planned.

Missing the development of the personal discipling ministries, some churches rely on organizational skills and platform expertise. This takes much invested effort while producing little lasting return.

Pity the church whose output is mechanically determined by its input. Even a perfect machine can put out no more than its input.

True edification, on the other hand, cooperates with the laws of life. Living seed invested in good ground *"bringeth forth, some an hundredfold, some sixty, some thirty"* (Matt. 13:23).

Nor can any amount of very spiritual public efforts care for all the needs of a church family. Thank God for any hopeful trends along this line, but there is yet more in His plans for us.

Still further, evangelism, whether public or personal, cannot see the church through to the quickening needed today. Scripture is very plain in requiring the average church member to be involved in strengthening other individuals in a personal manner.

THE SCRIPTURE TEACHES PERSONAL EDIFICATION

The New Testament presents a startling array of texts on this theme.

Passing by our Lord Jesus Christ's very personal ministry with numbers of individuals, let us move into the book of Acts and see how individual teaching, training, and exhortation played a vital part.

> *And how I kept back nothing that was profitable unto you, but have shewed you, and have taught you publickly, and from house to house* (Acts 20:20).

> *Therefore watch, and remember, that by the space of three years I ceased not to warn every one night and day with tears* (Acts 20:31).

The *New American Standard Bible* translates the last part of verse 31: *"I did not cease to admonish each one with tears."* So we see the apostle reached "every one" really by effort with individuals.

The same Greek words for "each one" are found in 1 Thessalonians 2:11, which Phillips translates:

You will remember how we dealt with each one of you personally, like a father with his own children, comforting and encouraging.

Imagine the apostle's heavy burden of work. Yet he could write to this young church and say, I have ministered to you one by one. The next verse reveals what he hoped to accomplish by this dealing with individuals:

We told you from our own experience how to live lives worthy of the God who is calling you to share the splendour of his own kingdom (1 Thess. 2:12, Phillips).

Here are other texts that set forth the same very personal ministry and also make abundantly clear that this is a work assigned to each believer.

Let us therefore follow after the things which make for peace, and things wherewith one may edify another (Rom. 14:19).

We then that are strong ought to bear the infirmities of the weak, and not to please ourselves. Let every one of us please his neighbour for his good to edification (Rom. 15:1-2).

And I myself also am persuaded of you, my brethren, that ye also are full of goodness, filled with all knowledge, able also to admonish one another (Rom. 15:14).

Whom we preach, warning every man, and teaching every man in all wisdom; that we may present every man perfect in Christ Jesus: whereunto I also labour, striving according to his working, which worketh in me mightily (Col. 1:28-29).

Let the word of Christ dwell in you richly in all wisdom; teaching and admonishing one another in psalms and hymns and spiritual songs, singing with grace in your hearts to the Lord (Col. 3:16).

Wherefore comfort one another with these words (1 Thess. 4:18).

Wherefore comfort yourselves together, and edify one another, even as also ye do.

And we beseech you, brethren, to know them which labour among you, and are over you in the Lord, and admonish you; and to esteem them very highly in love for their work's sake. And be at peace among yourselves.

Now we exhort you, brethren, warn them that are unruly, comfort the feebleminded, support the weak, be patient toward all men (1 Thess. 5:11-14).

Notice how the preceding passage clearly distinguishes between the leadership responsibilities and this more general obligation of mutual edification assigned to all members of the church.

For we hear that there are some which walk among you disorderly, working not at all, but are busybodies. Now them that are such we command and exhort by our Lord Jesus Christ, that with quietness they work, and eat their own bread. But ye, brethren, be not weary in well doing.

And if any man obey not our word by this epistle, note that man, and have no company with him, that he may be ashamed. Yet count him not as an enemy, but admonish him as a brother (2 Thess. 3:11-15).

Till I come, give attendance to reading, to exhortation, to doctrine (1 Tim. 4:13).

Preach the word; be instant in season, out of season; reprove, rebuke, exhort with all longsuffering

*and doctrine. For the time will come when they will
not endure sound doctrine; but after their own lusts
shall they heap to themselves teachers, having itching
ears* (2 Tim. 4:2-3).

*For a bishop must be blameless, as the steward of
God; not self-willed, (not soon angry) not given to
wine, no striker, not given to filthly lucre; but a lover
of hospitality, a lover of good men, sober, just, holy,
(temperate) holding fast the faithful word as he hath
been taught, that he may be able by sound doctrine
both to exhort and to convince the gainsayers. For
there are many unruly and vain talkers and deceivers,
specially they of the circumcision: whose mouths
must be stopped, who subvert whole houses, teaching
things which they ought not, for filthy lucre's sake*
(Titus 1:7-11).

Notice that the bishop, or elder-pastor, is told
how (v. 9) he is to overcome those whose words
are spreading error among individuals in the
congregation. The wholesome, defensive
weapon is authoritative, individual exhortation.
Continue now to the next chapter and note
God's chain of individual training: Paul to Titus,
Titus to mature women, mature women to
younger women. This kind of instruction is best
done in face to face encounters.

*But speak thou the things which become sound
doctrine: That the aged men be sober, grave, temperate, sound in faith, in charity, in patience. The aged
women likewise, that they be in behaviour as be-
cometh holiness, not false accusers, not given to
much wine, teachers of good things; that they may
teach the young women to be sober, to love their husbands, to love their children, to be discreet, chaste,
keepers at home, good, obedient to their own husbands, that the word of God be not blasphemed* (Titus
2:1-5).

This chapter contains much on individual exhortation. Study carefully verse 15:

These things speak, and exhort, and rebuke with all authority. Let no man despise thee.

See the authority that belongs to the personal edifier. Directly, however, the apostle moves on to caution Titus that such a ministering one must always be *"gentle, shewing all meekness unto all men"* (Titus 3:2).

Take heed, brethren, lest there be in any of you an evil heart of unbelief, in departing from the living God. But exhort one another daily, while it is called To day, lest any of you be hardened through the deceitfulness of sin (Heb. 3:12-13).

Notice here the effects of sin and what is God's instrument to prevent its malignancy from developing. Individual exhortation is the chosen tool.

And let us consider one another to provoke unto love and to good works: not forsaking the assembling of ourselves together, as the manner of some is; but exhorting one another: and so much the more, as ye see the day approaching (Heb. 10:24-25).

GOD'S PLAN FOR THE CHURCH INVOLVES PERSONAL EDIFICATION

God gives spiritual equipment to each believer. These gifts are manifested and used for the profit of all others. God does not always work with a vertical strike. One of the believers in your church may be having trouble simply because another believer has not exercised his equipment to benefit his brother. The troubled man may be calling on God and hoping for some heavenly visitation in his private praying, but

30

the real problem is in the life of a brother who does not minister to others as he should. There is the holdup.

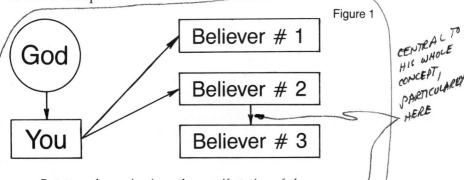

Figure 1

CENTRAL TO HIS WHOLE CONCEPT, PARTICULARLY HERE

> But to each one is given the manifestation of the Spirit for the common good (1 Cor. 12:7, NASB).

In figure 1, fellow believer Number 1 needs your help. Furthermore, believer Number 3 receives his needed encouragement, instruction, or added insights from Number 2, but this spiritual uplift might never take place if Number 2 receives no input from you. This is the nature of body life as expressed in Ephesians 4:16: "*The whole body . . . grows and builds itself up in love, as each part does its work*" (NIV).

> Now on the last day, the great day of the feast, Jesus stood and cried out, saying, "If any man is thirsty, let him come to Me and drink. He who believes in Me, as the Scripture said, 'From his innermost being shall flow rivers of living water.' " But this He spoke of the Spirit, whom those who believed in Him were to receive; for the Spirit was not yet given, because Jesus was not yet glorified (John 7:37-39, NASB).

A thoughtful study of this text will show that the Spirit Himself is the vital flow Jesus had in mind, as verse 39 indicates. Next, see that the believer's intake is mentioned in verse 37. Thirsting for comfort, refreshment, or the like, he comes to Christ, and he receives in the Spirit. Then in the next verse the Christian is shown as an intermediate supplier of vital edification to those beyond. Verse 38 depicts output. The believer therefore is a channel of the Spirit's work within Christ's assembly.

A little reflection makes clear that a channel can be blocked at either end. Many believers labor hard and long to get the input straightened out. They are much concerned about their life from God and wish to take in more from Him. However, we need to consider our output as well. By this, I do not mean routine religious work. Rather, it is essential that we make definite arrangement for a *spiritual* output that touches other lives directly. This outflow might take the form of kind words to a distressed one or perhaps practical suggestions to one bogged in indecision—all based on Scripture. In any case, the output must be of the same quality and quantity as the input. If not, something is clogging the works.

This is why I believe so much in personal edification and deeper involvement with fellow workers of the local body where we are. If we do not "dead-end" any truth but continually pour life and deeper truths into others, then we may expect God to be faithful in supplying more meaningful input to us. We will gain new insights into His depths as we serve. This means, in the matter of structuring a church in a spiritual way, leaders must see to it that members have such a meaningful output.

The average church member is grotesquely shriveled from lack of spiritual functioning. Repeatedly he is challenged to deepen his spiritual life with God. This is painfully futile, unless he is also offered deeper forms of expressing new life. It seems ludicrous to challenge a man to seek a deep spiritual experience on the input side of his life and then deprive him of any meaningful outlet.

[handwritten marginal note: GIFT/WORKS ARE ALSO A MEANS OF GRACE!]

Surely the Scriptures not only teach us how to obtain divine equipment and deeper spiritual power, but the Word also gives definite directions as to how we are to share this valuable intake. Individual admonition and upbuilding is an imperative for each life for the following reasons:

1. This upbuilding is God's plan for perfecting His church.
2. Such upbuilding, in both direct teaching and example, is found all through the Bible.
3. God's authority and His special blessings belong to those who practice personal admonition.

Each one must take in privately from another. Still further, you and I need the outflow to others. I need it, and my brother needs it.

May the church recover this forgotten art of personal edification.

3

Ready with a Word
in Season—
Spontaneous Edification

*The tongue of the wise makes
knowledge acceptable.
But the mouth of fools spouts
folly.
A man has joy in an apt answer,
And how delightful is a timely
word!* (Prov. 15:2,23, NASB).

*A perverse man spreads strife,
And a slanderer separates inti-
mate friends* (Prov. 16:28, NASB).

*Like apples of gold in settings
of silver
Is a word spoken in right cir-
cumstances.*

*Like an earring of gold and an
ornament of fine gold
Is a wise reprover to a listen-
ing ear* (Prov. 25:11-12, NASB).

More often than not, the seasonable word—
though it appears spontaneous—is a somewhat
prepared word. Powerful, life-changing admonition is not manufactured out in the traffic of per-

sonal encounters. It is stored in the heart during times of quiet.

Counseling may come forth spontaneously, but it rises from a heart prepared by thoughtful study of Scripture.

For an example of this use of the Bible, turn to 1 John 1:7.

But if we walk in the light, as he is in the light, we have fellowship with one another, and the blood of Jesus, his Son, purifies us from every sin (NIV).

This very useful verse at once impresses the mind with the promise of fellowship with one another and cleansing from all sin. A second look shows that these two blessings are the result of the meeting of a certain condition. The condition demanded is that of absolute honesty, a ridding ourselves of all deception. Sin must be faced openly, honestly—out in the light.

It is enlightening to notice the repeated phrase *"If we say"* in 1 John 1:6, 8, and 10. The inside alternate verses begin, *"But if we walk in the light"* (v. 7) and *"If we confess our sins"* (v. 9). Very obviously God is here making a marked distinction between two attitudes.

The careful presenting of these truths to an open heart is very effective in loosing one from deception. By going to the basic issue, personal sin, it also helps a man rid himself of insulation from his fellows.

If you are alone with a friend and have time, the careful discussion of the twin results promised in 1 John 1:7 to those who meet the condition of honest confession of sin will be profit-

36

able. Hold before the mind the promise of re-
stored fellowship and forgiveness—right with
God and right with man. Do not fail to go over
the basis of that divine reconciliation, the blood
of Jesus Christ, God's own Son. If possible, pray
with your friend, confessing sin and claiming
this offering.

There is a vast difference between flattery and **KEEPING**
encouragement, between angry lashing out and **BALANCE**
constructive reproof.

> *Faithful are the wounds of a*
> *friend,*
> *But deceitful are the kisses of*
> *an enemy* (Prov. 27:6, NASB).
>
> *It is better to listen to the re-*
> *buke of a wise man*
> *Than for one to listen to the*
> *song of fools* (Eccles. 8:5, NASB).

Many are wary of meddling in other people's
affairs and go to the opposite extreme of refusing
to help the needy. I believe there are more who
refuse to help than who meddle.

One who is not directly involved in a difficulty
often can see the way out quite clearly. A brief
word spoken in the Spirit will perhaps strike the
heart and turn the life upward again.

> *Let the righteous smite me in*
> *kindness [lovingly] and reprove me;*
> *It is oil upon the head;*
> *Do not let my head refuse it.*
> (Psalm 141:5, NASB).

37

If everyone within each church fellowship who should be *"able also to admonish one another"* (Rom. 15:14) were to begin doing so, new life would rise in the churches. Even when there is not time, occasion, or know-how to get to the root of a matter through more intensive counseling, a good word can help.

What I propose to do now is to reach into actual experience and relate a variety of cases that presented opportunities for counseling. For the most part, these are very ordinary examples where even the simplest word would make a difference.

EXAMPLE 1

"There is a meat grinder inside me."

The man who shot that curious expression in my direction was already passing out the church door. It had reference to his inner disturbance at the rather searching sermon. Grasping his hand momentarily, I took time for exactly three words: *"God* gives peace." I might have used actual Scripture, such as *"Peace* I *leave with you"* (John 14:27, author's emphasis).

By this short phrase of truth with emphasis on the word *God,* I intended to convey two basic truths: first, a warning that inner confusion surely does not come from God who makes peace, and second, a word of encouragement—He does provide peace.

As it turned out, my passing shot of truth, and prayer at home afterwards, came to fruition as my friend thought over things later that evening.

EXAMPLE 2

"I'm so depressed!" "I don't seem to get anything done."

38

It is normal to be depressed whenever there are neglected duties. We are made that way, or at least we should be. Help your friend to distinguish between other discouragements and those very normal despondencies that come from multiplied, undone tasks.

When appropriate, turn him tactfully to Proverbs 21:25:

> The desire of the slothful killeth him; for his hands refuse to labour.

Now ask him to find from this text a possible cause for depression. Perhaps help him make out a schedule of the troubling, undone tasks and then encourage his making progress reports.

"I can still be a Christian even though—" EXAMPLE 3

It is tragic that many beginners in the Christian life wobble and stagger before other Christians and are not given even obvious truths for their admonition. The above statement reflects the reasoning in some hearts bent on compromise.

At the very least, Matthew 6:24 should come to mind.

> No man can serve two masters: for either he will hate the one, and love the other; or else he will hold to the one, and despise the other. Ye cannot serve God and mammon.

Reinforce it with a statement such as "You can't serve both God and sin, self, or Satan. You must get both feet on the same side of the fence."

Remember, you do not have to come up with a counseling spectacular in order to change a life. Use the truth you have at hand.

EXAMPLE 4   "I've never had so many things go so wrong."

The only board the carpenter cuts is the one he intends to use. *"It is God which worketh in you both to will and to do of his good pleasure"* (Phil. 2:13).

Add words of your own such as "We often see signs along the road reading Men at Work. Well, you have over your life right now a sign that reads God at Work."

Along with these words you might choose to look at such texts as Psalm 138:8, Romans 8:28, or Ephesians 2:10.

EXAMPLE 5   "I simply can't make my mind up, so I'm trusting God to close the door if it's not right."

Here is passivity and deception of a common variety. Passively saying, "Thy will be done," may be an escape mechanism for dodging difficult decisions. Read this Scripture:

> *I will instruct you and teach*
> *you in the way which you*
> *should go;*
> *I will counsel you with My eye*
> *upon you.*
>
> *Do not be as the horse or as the*
> *mule which have no under-*
> *standing,*

*Whose trappings include bit
and bridle to hold them in
check* (Psalm 32:8-9, NASB).

According to verse 8, how does God make His will known to us?

Look at verse 9. What distinguishes you and me from the animal?

You see, God chooses to lead His children by enlightening their understanding. Do not require God to give providential pulls on the reins.

— Joe ?

Animals follow the open-and-closed-door method of leading, so to speak. If the corral gate is left open, they will usually "feel led" to go out. If it is closed, they are "led" to stay within. Let us not be that way.

"I am tempted to discouragement because there is so much weakness and sin in my life."   EXAMPLE 6

If this statement comes from one you know to be godly, it might be that 2 Corinthians 4:7 is the encouragement he needs.

But we have this treasure in jars of clay to show that this all-surpassing power is from God and not from us (NIV).

As Watchman Nee has pointed out, all of us need to make the double discovery suggested by this text. We vessels are very earthly indeed. But the treasure is glorious. No one can endure the revelation of the one without the other.

From this point of view, deeper disclosures of sin within might mean new love for the Lord. Study Luke 7:47.

41

EXAMPLE 7   "I'm going under!"

When this cry is real and comes from a numbing tragedy, it is no time for long expositions of high and mighty things. By all means grab him before he goes under.

Go with me now to visit a young couple whose long-awaited and only baby has died. We shall first read together this Scripture:

> *Trust in the Lord with all your heart,*
> *And do not lean on your own understanding.*
>
> *In all your ways acknowledge Him,*
> *And He will make your paths straight* (Prov. 3:5-6, NASB).

With all your heart now place this whole question in God's hands. Do not try to think it through. It is too much for our understanding. Only lean—lean on the Lord. Pray, and acknowledge Him as Lord.

Follow up this quick rescue approach by a later visit. After giving basic teaching on our resurrection hope in Jesus Christ and the comfort God offers, improve the situation by a positive challenge put in these words:

"Being hurt deeply is often the prelude to more meaningful prayer. Utter helplessness and prayerfulness seem to go together. I challenge you to begin a new life of prayer." Suggest steps and definite objectives.

"The Bible is all Greek to me."   EXAMPLE 8

Penetrate exceptional dullness by basic, simple questions directly from the Scripture. Turn to John 3:16 and work through the questions that follow.

For God so loved the world, that He gave His only begotten Son, that whoever believes in Him should not perish, but have eternal life (John 3:16, NASB).

1. According to the latter part of this verse, what is the wonderful destiny offered to us?
2. What is the other possible destiny?
3. What must we do to have eternal life?
4. Believe in whom?
5. What does it mean to believe *in* Him?
6. According to the first part of the verse, what is God's attitude toward the world?
7. How much does He love the world?
8. Why did our Lord go through all that?
9. Have you personally believed and received Him?

Such a use of the Bible tends to draw the truths deeply into the understanding and, it is to be hoped, brings about a quickening.

"I feel boxed in: there are so many rules."   EXAMPLE 9

"His commandments are not grievous" (1 John 5:3). God's fences do not block you from the right path. They hinder only trespassers.

Brief notes of Scripture points or diagrams such as the following are very helpful for defusing such a complainer.

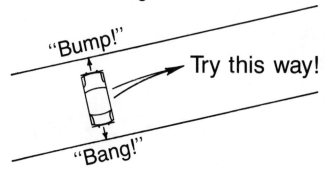

Figure 2   Feeling fenced in?

"Bump!"

Try this way!

"Bang!"

EXAMPLE 10   Approaching death: "I'm afraid!"
The only way to challenge deep shadows is with the light of truth. Darkness respects light. Never use inadequate carnal tools for this task. There is danger in giving a grieving loved one or a terminally ill patient artificial emotional stimulation. Later, the depths will look even blacker and in addition the sufferer will feel guilty.

The Scripture plainly prescribes what truths we are to use at such times and then commands, *"Comfort one another with* these *words"* (1 Thess. 4:18, author's emphasis). This refers to the great resurrection truths in the preceding verses. These should be read deliberately in the hearing of the distressed ones. Other Scriptures such as portions of 1 Corinthians 15 and Hebrews 2 should also be used.

Old familiar texts come alive at times like these. Do not forget Matthew 11:28-30 (NASB).

Come to Me, all who are weary and heavy-laden, and I will give you rest. Take My yoke upon you, and learn from Me, for I am gentle and humble in heart; and YOU SHALL FIND REST FOR YOUR SOULS. *For My yoke is easy, and My load is light.*

Observe how personally it is presented—as a conversation between the Lord and the grieving one. If applied personally, even the familiar Twenty-third Psalm can speak with new meaning.

The main thing is to make sure that you challenge the realm of darkness by standing in the authority of Jesus Christ. Study Colossians 1:13 with Hebrews 2:14-15. Be sufficiently bold. It is Christ's power exercised in believing prayer that will turn the tide.

Some situations, however, are peculiarly resistant to help. Failure is deep and repeated. We will go next to these special cases.

4

Special Help:
The Deliverance
Encounter

I have a riddle for you. Suppose a man has committed the same sin 499 times. He has confessed the sin 498 times. Now, what is the one thing this man really needs? (Stop and think it over a few moments before reading on.)

You may further suppose the man has made his confession as honestly as he knows how, even to the point of tears, and that he really wants to be free. Now what is it he needs? True enough, God requires that he make confession number 499. But God also offers something more than what he is experiencing. If not, then sin number 500 is surely coming up!

The poor man needs a kind of *deliverance encounter*. My reader, you might be the one to help such a person. Perhaps he needs converting, but for purposes of this chapter let us assume he is a believer.

Furthermore, the truths taught earlier in this book would likely fit this need. The trouble is that some are unable to grasp them because they are avoiding the showdown that genuine repentance requires.

Your personal help comes into the picture here. When a believer is deeply defeated in sin, it might be that a more dynamic personal assistance is the thing needed.

By "deliverance encounter" I do not mean some extraordinary, bombshell happening. Never employ the extraordinary when the ordinary will work. Stay as standard as possible. Keep presenting truths in their proper order. If they are received, they will generally bring release. Where there is no indication of the Spirit's blessings on your efforts, search to see if the truths are being appropriated. As long as a man is able to receive truth, he is responsible to appropriate and act on it.

Now let us proceed to develop a plan for loosing the bonds of personal sin from a struggling fellow believer who seems unable to make headway.

"YOU MEAN I AM LOST?"
The importance of making a correct appraisal of each particular case cannot be overemphasized.

Imagine for a moment that you face, as I once did years ago, a sobbing sailor. This man is racked in his conscience and explains his story somewhat as follows:

"I am a believer in Jesus Christ and attended a Bible School for a time before entering the service. A year ago I was married, and now I have fallen and have not been true to her. God knows how I have wept over this terrible mistake! I have pled with Him again and again to forgive me and make me know that He is still with me. In des-

48

peration I have been to the chaplain and also to the base psychiatrist. They both tell me that I tend to have a weakness in the sexual area of my life. My real problem, though, is that I am shortly leaving for overseas on a dangerous mission, and I need to know where I stand with God. I am so afraid and so upset in my heart."

Having said that, he bends double with racking sobs. Now, what will you say to this young man?

Dialogue with others who counsel leads me to realize that the sobbing friend will by most fellow counselors be given 1 John 1:9. After prayer, he will likely be sent out clinging to 1 Corinthians 10:13 for the future.

However, experience has shown me this treatment is far from adequate if the problem is as ingrained as the above-mentioned situation turned out to be. Something more is needed.

Look over his words again. Then read how I dealt with him.

"My friend, there is one thing wrong. Apparently you have not repented."

"What do you mean?" He gasped, and raised his head to look with wonderment at me.

"By your own words you have asked God to forgive you for your 'weakness' and your 'mistake,' but now I suggest that you repent of the sin of adultery."

Further questioning produced evidence of a lifelong pattern of immorality. His lips had claimed that he was a believer, but his life said otherwise. Which should be trusted? The sharp sword of God's Word can lay bare the true heart.

I continued: "Let us read, now, what God says

about your sin in 1 Corinthians 6:9-10. '*Or do you not know that the unrighteous shall not inherit the kingdom of God? Do not be deceived; neither fornicators, nor idolaters, nor adulterers, nor effeminate, nor homosexuals, nor thieves, nor the covetous, nor drunkards, nor revilers, nor swindlers, shall inherit the kingdom of God*' " (NASB).

His anguished cry interrupted, "You mean I am lost!"

"That is what is warned of here—unless one repents, and God has mercy on him. I know He will be merciful to you if you truly repent. Jesus says that His sheep will respond to His voice. If you are His, yield now to His will."

Without waiting for anything further, he began to pour out his heart to God. He made a definite confession of his sins by name, including not only adultery and his breach of vows but other lying and deception as well.

After this breakthrough, it was an easy matter to proceed with further steps to assure his deliverance.

Exactly what then is a "deliverance encounter?" It is simply a plan of more direct, personal help where ordinary words of encouragement or instruction might fail. Let us now go over the encounter in detail.

APPROACH If there is a pattern of repeated failure in sin, offer in a kind manner to share the burden.

Many times, however, the person himself will not be facing the real problem. This deception must be overcome. The source of defeat may be much deeper than the lesser matter that he admits.

It is important to notice carefully the person's attitude toward his sin. Does he speak of it with ease or difficulty? Is there desire or delight shown in discussing it? Worry? Torment? Does he feel isolated from the common stream of human experience? Is he languishing in the swamp? Defensive? Too objective? Perhaps well-practiced in divulging the matter to other counselors? Fearful and hopeless? Above all, does he see it as God sees it?

Here is the plan, step by step. It is best if more than one meeting is used to cover the steps.

What a vast difference there is between repentance and remorse.

> *Godly sorrow brings repentance that leads to salvation and leaves no regret, but worldly sorrow brings death* (2 Cor. 7:10, NIV).

This text might be a commentary on Peter and Judas. Both in effect denied Jesus, and both grieved. But Judas destroyed himself, whereas Peter reaffirmed his love to the Savior and led thousands to repentance as he preached the gospel in the very city where he had failed.

Grief over the dirt, hurt, or the evil results of sin is not enough. Tears are not necessarily significant. Bring the counselee to face frankly what God says. Where possible, read a Scripture that shows God's judgment of the very sin involved.

In prayer of definite repentance, naming the sin by name, claim the offered blood of Jesus for cleansing. Have the individual kneel with the

51

Bible open to a text such as 1 John 1:7 to be read as part of his prayer. Where necessary, the critical, showdown aspect of this prayer can be strengthened by including elements of the "battle prayer" outlined in chapter 10.

**SHOW HIM
A DELIVERING TRUTH**

Remember, proceed *graciously*, not *legalistically*. Rest obligations on provisions. That is, after gaining a definite break with the sin, lift the counselee by stressing what God has already done. Hold off all practical suggestions regarding his life and practices until the provisions of grace are clear to him.

The wonderful news is that no burden is now laid on the weakened, failing back. It is not that he needs to *do*; he needs to *know*. Tell him what Christ has already done for him. And, at least, show him John 8:36. Point toward the great truths of our identification with the Lord Jesus Christ (see chap. 7).

Now pray again, and this time claim what God provides. (Use one chosen text specifically.)

**GIVE
PRACTICAL HELPS**

1. Make needed restitution.
2. Set up a plan of private and public worship.
3. Revise daily schedule so as to avoid exposure to temptation.
4. Warn to expect continued pull, emotional letdowns.
5. Arrange follow-through meetings (wherein you must encourage, teach further, warn, lift up again, and hold on confidently now that the temptation's back has been broken).

Have him memorize and study such texts as HELP HIM TO RESIST THE DEVIL Ephesians 1:17-23, Colossians 2:9-10, 1 John 3:8, and Revelation 12:11.

If you sense that the problem is more dynamic than can be explained on the basis of the enemy tempting through the old carnality, then utilize principles concerning spiritual warfare taught in chapter 10.

Protect and cleanse yourself before and after PROTECT AND CLEANSE YOURSELF each session.

Hold on in prayer for the one counseled.

At times this approach does not succeed. It is WHEN THE ENCOUNTER DOES NOT DELIVER no cure-all. Unless there is some degree of willingness and understanding, no approach will succeed.

Man's volition is sacred. God made it so, and He does not violate it. What we could not do for ourselves, Christ did *in our stead*. Now, however, He works *in* us. There is to be a concurrence of our wills with His power. We are responsible to exercise choice and make intelligent appropriation.

Let us now investigate several cases that require an undeceiving before liberation can take effect.

"I don't understand what God is doing. He CASE 1 took away my problem with alcohol, and I am asking Him to break this other habit also, but it hangs on."

I must confess to shocking a few people of this type by saying, "Well, if that's the situation, let's get right down on our knees and tell God to get on the ball and not be holding back what you need." And then I usually add, "Or do you think the fault lies with you?" Each one has readily seen his deception.

Notice in the counselee's opening remarks that not once did he assume any accountability. To his mind, even the second habit was something happening to him rather than something he was doing repeatedly.

CASE 2   "I simply can't believe this has happened to me. Never before have I been involved in any serious sin like this. It was all so unexpected and happened so fast. Now my life is nearly ruined."

Here is another passive stance taken to excuse oneself from responsibility and blame. A really serious plunge into sin never comes all at once. According to 1 Corinthians 10:13, temptations are never of an uncommon sort.

> No temptation has seized you except what is common to man. And God is faithful; he will not let you be tempted beyond what you can bear. But when you are tempted, he will also provide a way out so that you can stand up under it (NIV).

We see here also that the faithfulness of God's character is presented as ground for our assurance of deliverance. If God is faithful, then escape is possible.

Chances are this fallen friend may have been indulging in some related sin over a long period of time. Thus, he weakened gradually. The devil will sometimes work patiently over many months or years in order to deal a knockout blow.

"This temptation is too much for me. It is so intense I simply cannot stand it much longer. Why doesn't God do something?" CASE 3

This is somewhat similar to the previous case, except that the allurement to evil is presented openly and more continually.

Again, we know that God has pledged that no one will be subjected to weird, overly intense abuse from the enemy. Probably the problem is that the man has a raw and exposed area in his life. He has given ground to the tempter. Or, putting it another way, he is sensitized to temptation because of toying with it.

"I really meant it that day when I prayed with you for my spiritual deliverance, but I soon found the old desires were there as strong as ever. I wonder if I will ever be free." CASE 4

Suppose you ascertain that this person truly has repented and has some understanding of the truths that help one to walk in liberty, especially those in Romans 6-8. Then it may be that this one slipped again simply from ignorance regarding a very common problem.

To be strongly tempted again is not necessarily to fall. Many a repentant soul is jarred by the realization that the old desire has not vanished. But that does not mean victory has not come.

Take an illustration. Suppose you crave chocolate candy, and someone offers you a box but

55

adds the warning that each chocolate contains arsenic. You look longingly at the candy but you have enough regard for the dreaded poison to forgo eating the chocolate. You see, then, it is not necessary to hate the chocolate in order to keep from the poison. Simply because you still like chocolate does not mean that you cannot be delivered from this fatal eating.

Remember, too, God can in time *"turn away mine eyes from beholding vanity; and quicken . . . me in thy way"* (Psalm 119:37). Then he can complete the alteration. *"Through thy precepts I get understanding: therefore I hate every false way"* (Psalm 119:104).

FURTHER OBSERVATIONS *"Except ye repent, ye shall all likewise perish"* (Luke 13:3). According to Jesus, repentance is an absolute requirement. If a man does not gain freedom after you have attempted to help him, the problem is likely to be here. Read together the first half of Ephesians 5, or use 1 John 1, and pray for full light to shine upon your moments of counseling together. Ask the Spirit to expose any deception.

If the repentance has been genuine, another hindrance might be in the matter of understanding our position in Christ. Teach this patiently and repeatedly until it is grasped. A final area to go over, if your friend is still not relieved, involves the follow-through and recovery phases. Make sure he is not being tricked by some simple matter, and that he is employing all the means God has offered him. Check again the final portion of the deliverance-encounter steps already given.

I must add a word of caution. Many today resort to a false kind of exuberant friendship when trying to help those who are deeply fallen. It seems to be the "in" thing to do. Maybe friendship-sharing is popular among men today, but it is not everything with God. Whom would you choose to perform your eye surgery for cataracts: a rather cold and efficient eye surgeon whom you did not know personally or the warm, friendly, neighborhood butcher?

I fear that some of the modern compulsion to identify so closely with those in need is actually harmful. It is like sitting beside the one with cataracts and mentioning that you too have the same problem of poor eyesight. "Let's share and take one another's hands." This is how the blind get near the ditches. God wants to find sighted shepherds who can help wandering sheep.

It is not necessary to have one eye closed in order to identify with those who sit in darkness. You do not even have to squint! Stand straight; keep in the light. Only love them as you help them. That is what God requires.

It will be recalled that this whole chapter has been one of special help. We return now to our general theme of basic assistance to fellow believers.

5

The ABC Lessons
of Personal Edification—
What They Are
and How to Use Them

*Stop judging by mere appearances, and make
a right judgment* (John 7:24, NIV).

Knowing how to reach where the other person
hurts is of immense importance. If you set your
heart and mind to devise a plan for accomplish-
ing this, two large benefits will be yours.

1. You will have permanent tools for helping
   others. You will know the spiritual trail along
   which you can lead a brother.
2. It will help you to *locate* him—to tell where he
   really is and to touch the basic need.

Remember, on occasion we all need assistance
from others to regain perspective or to rid ourselves of some speck in the eye.

When I mention a definite plan for Christian
growth, an objection is usually heard. "We are
not to be carbon copies of one another, are we?"
No, but there is some sense, some order to normal spiritual progress.

**THERE IS PATTERN
TO CHRISTIAN
GROWTH**

These levels, or steps, of inner development in our life with God are invaluable in checking and stimulating the lives of others.

> *And he said, so is the kingdom of God, as if a man should cast seed into the ground; and should sleep, and rise night and day, and the seed should spring and grow up, he knoweth not how. For the earth bringeth forth fruit of herself; first the blade, then the ear, after that the full corn in the ear* (Mark 4:26-28).

Studying this text leads one to see that wherever there is life there is some plan, or pattern, of growth—from seed to full ear. God is a God of order.

If you can with some degree of certainty sit beside a poor derelict on the park bench and, using the so-called ABC steps of evangelism, bring him from hell to heaven, then how much more certain is it that you can be helpful to one who is already a brother in Christ.

While it is true there is only one Savior, it is also true there is great variety in conversion experiences. If ABC steps are legitimate in personal evangelism, it is fitting that we should discover and use God's ordered steps for Christian growth as we help one another. Do you know them?

Generally, whatever you know yourself you should be able to share with another person. Years ago, I went through a long period of careful reflection over what had been transpiring in my own spiritual life. Slowly, I came to see that there had been a definite growth pattern.

I might add that it had been "while men slept," for there had been few, if any, along life's way who had inquired about my soul's welfare. I

60

then determined that I would not leave my own children nor the believers about me to the same protracted struggles if I could help it. To my great delight I soon discovered that some of the lessons that had required many years for me to grasp were learned quickly by others when they had a bit of personal help.

Once I knew where to head, I found it much easier to have a marked effect on other lives as I spoke with them from an open Bible.

WHAT THEN ARE THE ABC LESSONS OF EDIFICATION?

These lessons really indicate levels of spiritual growth. They also may be thought of as a prescribed route over which you would take a son, daughter, or Christian friend whom you would assist spiritually. Finally, this list may serve as an index for discovering where one is bogged down. That is, you can soon determine what lesson is next due.

Here are the lessons for individual development:

1. A more serious view of sin
2. Our identification with Christ
3. The filling of the Holy Spirit
4. My place in the local church
5. The spiritual warfare
6. A life of intercession

Now you will deduce that if a person has not gotten to level 1, but is one of those half-hearted, coasting Christians, there will be hardened indifference. Of course, many of these individuals are very dutiful and active in religious works.

There will not be, however, a true responsiveness to the Lord and His fellowship.

Let us go a step further. Suppose a man has been brought into this first level of experience through a new working of the Holy Spirit but does not yet see and experience the second truth listed above. What will he be like? Will he not be discouraged and depressed?

The second growth lesson involves understanding not only how Christ died for me, but also that I died with Him and rose with Him. Can you explain the seeming contradiction between Colossians 3:3 and 3:5? How did we die with Christ? In what sense are we still having to put to death? When did verse 3 take place? How does verse 5 take place? Of course Romans 6-8 is the basic passage here, along with other texts as 2 Corinthians 5:14-21 and Galatians 5.

Suppose, however, even a man with these truths in his heart finds the spiritual life beginning to be a dry, hard pull for him. Chances are he needs to know that our union with Christ is meant to bring us the benefits of the Holy Spirit's fullness in our lives. Acts 2:32-33 needs to be studied and even diagrammed (Fig. 5, p. 88) Note the route the Holy Spirit takes to reach us. Now our Representative is in glory to share this supreme gift with us. Jesus' great ministry in mediation not only rids us of sin but provides us with the blessed Spirit (see Gal. 3:14). The body has full rights to all our exalted Head receives on our behalf.

Believers are all baptized by the Spirit (1 Cor. 12:13), but His filling is not automatic, and there-re we are commanded to exercise our will and avail ourselves of it (Eph. 5:18). The filling of the Spirit is normal, but I say again it is not automatic.

Next, if you discover one who is quite a "deeper life buff" and yet is either somewhat frustrated or a bit too independent in his attitude, I would then question whether he is a vital part of an assembly of believers. Perhaps he has not moved on to this step in his spiritual pilgrimage.

A man needs to know what his life-ministry is to be. Scripture teaches that each believer is to exercise the particular spiritual equipment God has given him. This is more than natural talent (Romans 12; 1 Cor. 12-14; Eph. 4; 1 Pet. 4:10-11).

Now, a man might have achieved all the foregoing levels of insights and development and still be erratic, compulsive, and perhaps depressed. Some apparently mature and experienced Christians are very flammable and difficult to predict. At times they seem driven. It could be that they have yielded certain areas to Satan's control. Perhaps they have little knowledge of how to resist and war against the enemy. This is disastrous. Satan has many more designs on us than getting us to "come on and do this bad thing." Study John 14:30; 2 Corinthians 2:11; and Ephesians 4:27. According to these texts, what is Satan really trying to gain?

Finally, one should develop a life of true intercessory prayer, the sooner the better. Probably the struggles in the earlier progress will spur him to deepen his prayer life. Happy the Christian with a friend who knows how to pray and how to put some of the secrets into words. Ob-

63

viously this has to be done with discretion. But how refreshing and helpful it is to have someone put a hand on your shoulder and point you into a life of prayer.

Charting the whole scheme of things could provide a layout as follows:

Lesson Needed for Next Level of Growth	Trouble Symptoms Indicating One Is Bogged Down at a Particular Stage of Progress
(Conversion)	Indifferent—Satisfied—Unconcerned
1. A MORE SERIOUS VIEW OF SIN	Discouraged—Defeated
2. OUR IDENTIFICATION WITH CHRIST	Dry—Tending Toward Old Defeats Again
3. THE FILLING OF THE HOLY SPIRIT	Frustrated—or Too Independent
4. MY PLACE IN THE LOCAL CHURCH	Compulsive—Erratic—Driven
5. THE SPIRITUAL WARFARE	Continuing Dullness— Moving with "Burdened Step."
6. A LIFE OF INTERCESSION	

Every believer desperately needs help from fellow believers in making these lessons a reality in his life. Each one of us must pass this way. The counselor himself is no exception. Having now completed an overview, let us take up in more detail each step of the scheme. As you proceed, remember the importance of discerning which lesson is next due in one's growth.

6

Lesson One:
A More Serious
View of Sin

Indifference is the shield behind which serious sin develops. Where there is spiritual unconcern there is undoubtedly little understanding of basic truths, nor will enlightenment come until there is somewhat of a personal showdown with sin.

Because men hold a light view of their sin, they not only continue marching toward disaster, but their very attitude disarms the edifiers who might otherwise help. Imagine a patient in the deadly grip of a malignancy smiling winsomely at the doctor, and the physician in turn thinking, *It couldn't be as bad as I suspected.* Then, returning the smile, the specialist cancels the date for the man's surgery. This mutual response would be lethal.

Unconcern will clog any spiritual artery. A more serious view of the entire issue of sin is evidence of rising spiritual vitality and precedes a new appetite for spiritual truth. We have already stated that edification, or true spiritual upbuilding, begins here.

THE FIRST STEP MUST BE FIRST   Suppose you are concerned for a Christian friend who spends all his time in business, pleasure, or some superfluous interest. You want to help him, so you make the approach, "Jim, you seem to spend too much time on the lake with your new boat. We miss you at church, and what about the spiritual life of your family?"

All of that might be well and good, but keep in mind that you are dealing with only a surface symptom. Needling Jim about these superficial evidences of his deeper need will not put the ax to the root. Somebody needs to help him—not only to make changes in his life-style but to be different in his heart.

This is where true personal edification comes in. In God's ball game, so to speak, no one gets to second base without tagging first. It is a first essential that careless believers take a more serious view of their sin for their own good and for the good of the family of God with whom they live.

Many sins have status among modern, respected people, but in reality they represent a communicable malignancy. The entire assembly of believers needs to be protected from those the apostle Peter warned of as "*having eyes full of adultery, and that cannot cease from sin; beguiling unstable souls: an heart they have exercised with covetous practices; cursed children* (2 Pet. 2:14). Paul wrote of those who "*fill up their sins alway: for the wrath is come upon them to the uttermost*" (1 Thess. 2:16).

Immediately we see from these words that sin always carries with it the tendency to increase, to apply the death grip on its victim. If done slowly, it is nevertheless done surely. A numbing carelessness regarding popular sins and the neglect of spiritual duties are a part of the problem. Apparently sin is in style, but that does not make it less evil.

Often popular sin spreads like wildfire among nearby people. The demons cooperate, while believers fail to help one another. In many bodies the protective white corpuscles are in short supply.

Here is a church family. The man is driving himself to make still more money. Home life is abandoned. His wife sees no fulfillment in domestic responsibilities. The children give vent to hateful temper, and the evil thus expressed becomes more entrenched. The once diligent mother yields to slackness, until whole days slip by in meaningless sloth.

Next, these conditions expose the victims to still other evil habits. At the last, the will lies chained in some secret dungeon. Modern church life will not rise very high for very long until some of these shackles are dealt with. Once in a great while God may send an earthquake, as with Paul and Silas, and shake all the prison doors open and loose all the chains. But He is today blessing those who will go to individuals one at a time and help them get free. There is a key of truth for every personal padlock.

No Christian will get on with God until he has a deeper showdown with sin. Here are some general suggestions for helping a friend with this experience.

How to Get to First Base

67

SUGGESTION 1 Do not rattle about in the twigs and branches of a person's need. Turn with him to Scripture that mentions basic sins by name, such as Galatians 5:19-21. Notice that the various terms are given in groups or categories.

> *Now the deeds of the flesh are evident, which are: immorality, impurity, sensuality, idolatry, sorcery, enmities, strife, jealousy, outbursts of anger, disputes, dissensions, factions, envyings, drunkenness, carousings, and things like these, of which I forewarn you just as I have forewarned you that those who practice such things shall not inherit the kingdom of God* (Gal. 5:19-21, NASB).

A helpful list from this text might be arranged as follows:
1. Sexual sins—immorality, impurity, sensuality
2. Religious evils—idolatry, sorcery
3. Relational sins or wrong attitudes—enmities, strife, jealousy, outbursts of anger, disputes, dissensions, factions, envyings
4. Sins of indulgence—drunkenness, carousings.

SUGGESTION 2 Draw the individual to see God's view of his sin by sharing His judgment of the same as recorded in Galatians 5:21. Similar texts with which you should be familiar are 1 Corinthians 6:9-10 and Ephesians 5:3-7. All of these are addressed to church people and make clear that no man can safely coast along in his sin. Those who are willfully breaking God's laws would be hard pressed to prove that they are Christians. *"The tree is known by his fruit,"* taught Jesus (Matt. 12:33). The fruit that God's Spirit produces in

His true child is not that of Galatians 5:19-21 but is that spoken of in Verses 22 and 23. Furthermore, *"They that are Christ's have crucified the flesh with the affections and lusts"* (Gal. 5:24).

Now make clear to your friend that he stands at the fork in the road and must repent. Point out that the above texts allow only two alternatives: no to sin and yes to God or else no to God and yes to sin. SUGGESTION 3

Have him pray in definite repentance with you. Then conclude by sharing atonement verses from Hebrews 10, for example. The deliverance-encounter approach outlined in chapter 4 might be necessary in cases of deeply entrenched, habitual sins.

Ideally, the person ought to be involved in more than a single passing discussion of this large subject of a more serious view of sin. Where there is time to go deliberately into the doctrine of sin, a deeper conviction might be stirred. **DEEPENING THE CONVICTION**

Few believers are clear in their understanding of this doctrine. There are three distinct aspects of the total sin problem:

1. Legal guilt or condemnation (Rom. 3:9-10; Gal. 3:22)
2. Inner defilement and tendencies toward evil (Rom. 7:17)
3. Wrong actions—omission and commission (James 4:17; 1 John 3:4).

In the above passages, the word *sin* is used with marked distinctions in meaning. In place of the term *sin* in each text, try substituting the descriptive terms I suggest. Then try to transpose the terms. You will see it simply cannot be done. Think a while over this until the implication becomes very clear.

Sin, then, is not only an action, but also a condition. What we *do* comes out of what we *are*. And we are fallen, corrupted beings because of the blight justly resting on us. We are all guilty—born in this state and with no merit before God. Quite obviously, how we view sin will deeply affect how we view and appreciate and appropriate the atonement of our Lord Jesus Christ.

A Christian's legal guilt is entirely cared for the moment he comes to the Savior. *"There is therefore now no condemnation to them which are in Christ Jesus"* (Rom. 8:1).

Turn now to Romans 4:5: *"But to him that worketh not, but believeth on him that justifieth the ungodly, his faith is counted for righteousness."* While it is true that God justifies the ungodly, He surely does not intend that His children live in their former, sinful condition. *"What shall we say then? Shall we continue in sin, that grace may abound? God forbid"* (Rom. 6:1-2 a).

As soon as one's record of damnation is cleared in heaven, the Spirit of God begins His work to remove defilement from the life. The very inner force of sin must be dealt with. As it is put to death, behavior changes.

God's records are not seen by human eyes. They are indicated in the experience and life of the person. *"Either make the tree good, and his fruit good; or else make the tree corrupt, and his fruit corrupt: for the tree is known by his fruit"* (Matt. 12:33).

Once these serious facts about sin fasten their grip on the formerly indifferent heart, an unmistakable stirring of spirit will begin. It is to be hoped this stirring will become a restlessness that refuses to be quieted except by still more truth.

7

Lesson Two:
Our Identification
with Christ

The believer who has been brought to take step 1 in receiving personal edification will be discouraged and defeated unless he is directly given other truth. Such a one is now ready for the precious teaching regarding how God views those who are in His Son.

It is a common experience with believers that the first blush of conversion fades upon discovering the power of the old life still lurking in the desires of the heart. Indeed, these desires usually refuse to be put down.

Caught in this uncomfortable straddle, some use the Bible texts promising eternal security to believers as a cushion to make sin more comfortable. Others, trying to rationalize from experience, conclude, None is perfect. Thus they intend to be less than perfect, and this degree of rebellion tends to rule out any real victory.

Sooner or later every effort to shore up the troubled conscience gives way, and the dark billows of discouragement take their toll.

There are, then, certain dark feelings that come from enlightenment regarding sin. This is not contradictory; it is necessary.

The person who has gotten this far in his spiritual progress ought not to be hit with a list of evangelical duties. At this point what he needs more than anything else is to be shown a delivering truth. Enforcing obligation and exposing one's failure in taking moral and spiritual responsibility are tools to use on the indifferent. After there is repentance, the wise personal edifier will lay these by and lift the downcast heart with teachings of God's gracious provisions.

And ye shall know the truth, and the truth shall make you free (John 8:32).

The most basic teaching to use in helping one out of defeat by sin is that of our identification with Jesus Christ. I will now suggest various ways of approaching and explaining this truth. (Let me strongly urge you to make use of the diagrams included and also to put key phrases in writing as you attempt to instruct one in this area of doctrine.)

Turn to 1 Corinthians 15:45.

And so it is written, The first man Adam was made a living soul; the last Adam was made a quickening spirit.

Here Adam is called "the first man," and Jesus is called "the last Adam." This can be illustrated by a line of figures all bearing the likeness of fallen, sinful Adam. After his sin, he bore the stoop of sin, and so do all members of his worldwide family.

It is amazing that Jesus was born into this family and bore its likeness. Read Romans 8:3, where we are told: "*God [sent] his own Son in the likeness of sinful flesh."* Note *"in the likeness of."* Though Jesus did no sin, he nonetheless bore the apparent stoop of our troubled condition.

Jesus is said to be "the last Adam." See Him at the end of the "Old Man" lineup (fig. 3). Now, our Lord not only was like us fallen ones, but also He took our guilt into His own body and suffered punishment in our place. In this sense He is said to be the *last* of sinful men. We were all executed (punished for sins) via our Substitute.

All who believe in Jesus Christ, whether living before or after His earthly ministry, are counted by God as having died with and in Christ. For us, our place in Adam's line ended at Calvary.

But that is not all. First Corinthians 15 goes on to point out in verse 47 that Jesus is also *"the second man."* He became that to us when He arose from the dead. From Mary's womb issued *"the last Adam,"* but the tomb was the womb of *"the second man."*

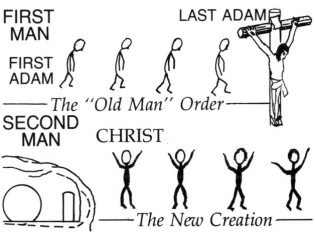

FIRST MAN

LAST ADAM

Figure 3

FIRST ADAM

——— *The "Old Man" Order* ———

SECOND MAN CHRIST

——— *The New Creation* ———

Look at the complete picture above. The risen Savior now heads a new race of men. We become part of this new order, or new creation, when we believe in Christ. God counts us in this new lineup—forever joined to Jesus Christ. Out of Adam—into Christ.

Consider carefully. If we have this new, raised-up-from-the-dead life, then we must be like our file Leader. The Old Man must go. Our New Man must take over—a new creation living out of God's gracious provisions!

HELP BELIEVERS DISTINGUISH BETWEEN PROVISIONS AND OBLIGATIONS

Many Christians are bowed in discouragement because they misunderstand basic truth. On the one hand, they struggle futilely to gain the position before God that Christ already provides so freely. On the other hand, they strive to convince themselves that their marked failures in obedience are to be remedied by a kind of deeper-life mental gymnastics. "I am dead to sin," they keep telling themselves. "Thus I am not responsive to it."

The misunderstanding here is fatal. Such a man is striving to be what God already declares him to be in Jesus Christ. In addition, failing to obey God in areas of Christian obligation, he substitutes a futile effort to believe Christ has somehow done this in his experience. Faith never makes something true that is not true.

Much benefit can be gained by meditating carefully on what Christ did *for* us (in our stead) as distinguished from what Christ must yet do *in* us. Two thousand years ago He did His work on our behalf and paid the price for all God's gracious provisions. In the present, He is working in us.

76

A simple procedure that has proved helpful to me is to write on a slip of paper the words *obligations* and *provisions*. Now ask the friend you are helping to say which of these terms is the more basic in God's plan of grace. Which is the root, and which is the fruit? Do we fulfill certain obligations and thus gain God's provisions? Or is it the other way around—we accept His provisions and thus are enabled to fulfill the obligations?

Obviously, the order of grace is: God's provisions are laid down first, and only by standing on that basis do we gain strength to obey and fulfill obligations.

Take another sheet of paper and strike a line down the middle. At the top of the left-hand side write "Provisions." "Obligations" then goes over the other column. Now, turn to Colossians 3 and proceed with the following progression of questions and statements.

At verse 3, underscore "you died" and "with Christ."

> For <u>you died,</u> and your life is now hidden <u>with Christ</u> in God (Col. 3:3, NIV).

Now dropping down to verse 5, underscore "put to death."

> <u>Put to death,</u> therefore, whatever belongs to your earthly nature; sexual immorality, impurity, lust, evil desires and greed, which is idolatry (Col. 3:5, NIV).

Go over in order these questions: According to verse 3, what died? When did this death occur? How do you explain the seeming contradiction between verse 3 and verse 5? (First we are told that we Christians are dead indeed, and next we are told that we have yet to experience a putting to death and are to get on with it.)

I suggest to you who would help others that you first go over these questions and write down your own answers. Then, go over my answers below.

What died? According to Colossians 3:3, *I* died. Now this answer cannot be improved on. Let it stand just as the Word here says it. We are *not* told that my sin nature died, my sins died, or any part of me died. It is simply stated that I died in my representative, Jesus Christ.

When did this death occur? If I died with Him, then this occurred when He died. That was two thousand years ago. True, it becomes real to me when I am born anew, but God counts that I died when Jesus died.

The next test comes when you attempt to put into words how it is that the believer is dead (verse 3) and yet faces the obligation to put to death the workings of his sinful nature (verse 5). This is not, of course, a contradiction; in one sense we are already dead, and in another we are still too much alive.

In Christ we are dead, but in our actual experience we are yet alive to the allurements of sin and thus are called on to put to death evil tendencies and appetites.

Which of these verses (3 or 5) is stated as a provision? (That is, in which are we simply informed of what Jesus Christ has done for us?) And which is stated as a command or obligation?

What is the significance of "therefore" in verse 5? It harks back to verse 3 and establishes the order of the whole teaching. The thrust of this section is: You are dead with Christ, *therefore* put to death. Provisions are laid down as the basis, and we are "therefore" instructed to fulfill the obligation of calling a halt to the rule of sin over us.

Another verse that might be studied with great profit is 2 Corinthians 5:14.

> *For Christ's love compels us, because we are convinced that one died for all, and therefore all died* (NIV).

Teaching this verse is a rewarding experience. Here the apostle tells us the secret for a life motivated by Christ's love.

Can you say with Paul, "Christ's love compels [me]"? You will be able to say this when you reach the conviction to which he came. Read the remainder of the verse again. Special illumination of the Spirit seems required to see the depth of that statement: *"[If] One died for all, then all died"* (Amp.).

Write the two halves of this special proposition, one beneath the other:

> *"[If] One died for all,*
> *then all died."*

Underscore *"if"* and *"then."* These words indicate that if the first statement is true, then the second follows. Next, circle *"One"* and *"all."* If One were the stand-in for all, then all died when He died. That is, we believers died by proxy in Jesus Christ. If He is our duly appointed representative, then God counts us as having been executed for our sins. That is precisely what happened at Calvary.

79

It may be true that I have not yet put to death sin in my experience as I ought. But, it is quite true nevertheless that I died via my substitute, Jesus Christ.

These Scriptures might be lined up on the provisions-obligations chart you began earlier, as indicated in the following diagram.

PROVISIONS	OBLIGATIONS
(to be received, believed, claimed)	(to be obeyed)
"You died . . . with Christ" therefore (Col. 3:3, NIV)	"Put to death" (Col. 3:5, NIV).
"[If] *One* died for *all,* then *all died.*" (2 Cor. 5:14, Amp., author's emphasis).	
"Our old man is crucified with Him . . . that henceforth	we should not serve sin." (Rom. 6:6).

We have seen thus far that Christ did not die simply to free us from sin's penalty but also to break sin's absolute power over us. Turn now to the most important of all the scriptural sections on this theme—Romans 6. Here is set forth the basis for victory over sin, namely, our identification with Christ. God accepts Him on our behalf. We are counted in Him.

See Romans 6:6. Even though we are descendants of Adam, God considers that connection officially ended. In that regard, we were executed via our Substitute two thousand years ago (see provisions-obligations chart).

Allow me to go over the same ground once more.

How do you explain the apparent contradiction between Colossians 3:3 and 3:5? The third verse says we are in one sense already dead; the fifth verse says that in another sense it is not yet so, but we are responsible to see that a dying takes place.

Notice the former is announced as a *provision*. Since Jesus was our substitute, God counts Calvary's crucifixion as having happened to us. Verse 5 is a command, but the *obligation* is based upon the *provision* (note "therefore").

Always bear in mind that God deals with us according to *grace*, not law. Thus, His provisions enable us to fulfill our obligations (see provisions-obligations chart). God first informs us, "I have done thus and so for you"; then follows the command, "You can and must therefore do thus and so."

OPENING THE UNDERSTANDING

An unyielding dullness often chokes the understanding of the one you wish to help in this area of the Christian life. To break through that, you must be simple, practical, and spiritual. Our weapons, or tools, are adequate only if we use them.

Prayer is very important. Pray with your friend as you begin the time of instruction and exhortation. After you have talked a while, stop and pray again that God will give His illumination. Pray also after the session. It might be especially helpful to make definite suggestions so that the counselee will pray to the point. Then both of you kneel. After this, teach him how to pray on his own, asking that God Himself will open his understanding.

On occasion, I write down the basic truths of Romans 6—not a weighty outline but simple statements from the key verses. Then I instruct the individual to take the paper home, compare it with the Scripture, and pray for the Holy Spirit to give understanding. Often, he will return, seeing!

The apostle Paul relied on prayer to bring about illumination to believers. Apparently, he was ever optimistic and thankful while so engaged:

> *Wherefore I also, after I heard of your faith in the Lord Jesus, and love unto all the saints, cease not to give thanks for you, making mention of you in my prayers; that the God of our Lord Jesus Christ, the Father of glory, may give unto you the spirit of wisdom and revelation in the knowledge of him: the eyes of your understanding being enlightened; that ye may know* (Eph. 1:15-18).

This experience of opening understanding is like a dawning of light. The gradual steps of comprehension might be listed progressively as:

1. Christ died for us.
2. Christ died for *me*.
3. Christ died on my behalf as my substitute.
4. I therefore died and rose with Him.
5. I may now claim this freedom from sin, and His new resurrection life, in my daily experience.

Keep a heart of hope as you attempt to share these teachings. Do not write them off as dif-

ficult "deeper life" matters only. They belong to
all God's children. You may have the assistance
of the Holy Spirit in sharing them.

Now we have received, not the spirit of the world,
but the spirit which is of God; that we might know
the things that are freely given to us of God (1 Cor.
2:12).

That chapter closes assuring us "we have the
mind of Christ." Thus, the divine outlook belongs to us. It is desperately needed at this
juncture in Christian experience and should be
prayed for resolutely.

Looking back, we discover two distinct steps
in God's plan of spiritual enlightenment:

First, the Lord begins to grip the understanding
with the fact that our sin condition is serious
and seemingly unconquerable.

Next, He ends that agony, which in many cases
is long-standing, by further enlightenment.
Often this needed insight comes as a friend
relates the truth about Jesus Christ—our place
in Him and His life in us.

However, the road up and out does not end
here. There is much more.

8

Lesson Three: The Filling of the Holy Spirit

It is a well-known fact that many a believer masters the two lessons of growth we have already covered and still runs out of steam. Things begin to get very dull and dry. Repeatedly he tries to recover the feelings once derived from the precious truths of our identification with Jesus Christ. Despite his best efforts, the tendencies toward the old defeats begin returning in strength.

It may be that you or one of your friends is in this exact position. Often what is now needed is a third level of edification, comprising a more definite understanding of the Holy Spirit's personal ministry.

In helping a brother who has a serious view of sin, is striving to live a godly life, and is yet failing, how do you proceed? First, ask questions in the area of our identification with Christ as covered in the preceding chapter. Question him over key verses of Romans 6 and other texts already cited. If he seems solid in his understanding and active in his appropriation of these truths, then you might observe that in all his talking he has not mentioned the Holy Spirit.

Turn to Romans 8:13 and ask: "According to this verse, what is the instrument by which we are to put to death our defeating sin?" We now are at the place where it must become clear that what God does for us—on our behalf, in Christ—He also desires to do *in* us by the Holy Spirit.

"Do you think of the Holy Spirit as a real person?" I frequently use this question with discouraged people. Be sure you resist the urge to qualify and explain the inquiry. Let it hang there, as is, before the mind. Remain quiet as your friend reaches for an answer.

Of course, the only answer to the question is yes—and it should be a comfortable yes. If needed, instruction might be given somewhat as follows:

God is a three-person Being. Man is a single-personality being. (Surely it is not surprising that God is different from man.) There is one God. He is not three different beings. However, it is proper to think of the three Persons (Father, Son, and Holy Spirit) as distinct—distinct Persons and yet unified in the one God. Our God is a triunity. The Father loved the world and gave the Son. The Son took on a body of flesh, died, and rose for us. The Holy Spirit now ministers within us.

It does not dishonor God to speak simply about Him. Revelation is not confusion. Rather, it is God's attempt to reach us where we are. He often puts very high truths in the bottom drawer where the least of us can reach. Holding this to be true and having struggled many years with people who had very vague notions of the

Spirit's personal influence in their lives, I have dared to use simple drawings such as this one:

ONE GOD

3 PERSONS

ONE BEING

Note: God is not three and yet one in the same manner. There is no contradiction. He is one *Being*, three *Persons*.

It might be helpful at this juncture to briefly look at Acts 2:32-33:

> God has raised this Jesus to life, and we are all witnesses of the fact. Exalted to the right hand of God, he has received from the Father the promised Holy Spirit, and has poured out what you now see and hear (NIV).

This very important Scripture might be diagrammed as follows:

The alignment suggested in this Scripture is quite significant. Jesus Christ not only mediates in the removal of our sin, but He is there as mediator as we receive the Spirit. He is indeed the Christ. The Anointed One is the Anointer—the Baptizer with the Spirit. Keep Him in His place. It is the Christ in glory who shares the supreme gift of the Spirit with us.

Now study 1 Corinthians 12:13.

Figure 5

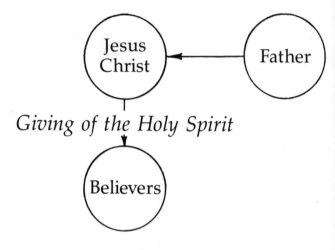

Giving of the Holy Spirit

> *For we were all baptized by one Spirit into one body—whether Jews or Greeks, slave or free—and we were all given the one Spirit to drink* (NIV).

We are now prepared to make the following addition to the provisions-obligations chart (p. 80):

Provisions	Obligations
"All baptized by one Spirit"	"Be filled,"
(1 Cor. 12:13, NIV, author's emphasis)	(Eph. 5:18)

Notice opposite the *provided* baptism is the command to be filled. Nor is this a difficult, extraordinary obligation. Filling may be ours quite simply and serenely because of the adequate provision of our gracious God.

Let me now illustrate the filling of the Holy Spirit. Obviously, this will be technically inadequate, but it is practically useful and, in defense, remember the Scriptural terms *baptism* and *filling* also carry very physical and concrete connotations. Both these terms as well as my illustration must be taken figuratively.

Figure 6

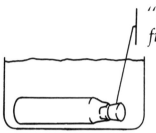

"Stoppers" preventing filling might be:

1. ignorance
2. fall into sin
3. neglect as time passes

Note: The vessel is in the element, yet not filled. Infilling will be normal when hindrances (stoppers) are removed. New challenges or additional obstacles create the need for a believer's new filling of the Holy Spirit. The apostles' repeated fillings in the first chapters of Acts demonstrate this point. Being filled with the Spirit provides God's special help when one specially needs it.

Clearly, new fillings of the Spirit will be required as a result of any of the "stoppers" listed on the diagram. For example, if one does not understand his need to be filled or has marked areas of ignorance concerning the Holy Spirit's work within his life, then new teaching is necessary, and a definite appropriation should follow.

As you move into these teachings be prayerful, be respectful, but dare to be simple and clear. Remember, great truths about God are not demeaned so much by simple handling as by making them into proud complexities. There is a time and place for everything. When you face a

faltering Christian, it is time for practical help—
not for a course in systematic theology.

Bad skips in living come from misunderstanding truth. Find the truth your friend needs to know and point it out clearly. Leaving him with brief notations or diagrams will be of great help in calling it to mind.

Study now the various events mentioned in John 7:39. Mark each of them and arrange them in some chronological fashion.

> On the last and greatest day of the Feast, Jesus stood and said in a loud voice, "If a man is thirsty, let him come to me and drink. Whoever believes in me, as the Scripture has said, streams of living water will flow from within him." By this he meant the Spirit, whom those who believed in him were later to receive. Up to that time the Spirit had not been given, since Jesus had not yet been glorified (John 7:37-39, NIV).

Notice the order:

1. Jesus raised from the dead and glorified at the right hand of the Father
2. The general giving of the Holy Spirit
3. Personal faith
4. Individual reception of the Spirit
5. And, from verse 38, the sharing of the Spirit's blessing with others.

At this point refer back to figure 1. Look again at verse 37. The drink referred to, according to verse 39, is the Holy Spirit. That which drives us to the Lord Jesus is nothing but our thirst. Christians should not be unduly shocked to find themselves wobbly, weak-kneed, and having to make repeated cries to the Lord. We are not to sin willfully but, on the other hand, we will never outgrow spiritual thirst. Our Lord intends for us to live inclined toward Him. We will not get far from His gate if He has His way. Driven as it were by our need, we will be found there knocking again and again.

The accuser literally devastates many a sensitive soul as he raises a weakened hand to knock again at the Lord's door. Here is where counsel comes in. Bring back perspective and tell him this is God's plan. Above all, present as normal the filling of the Holy Spirit.

Then go further. Help the individual to know that every principle in body life demands that outflow follow this inflow (John 7:38).

A word of caution is now in order. A fresh working of God's Spirit in one's life does not remove the need for further growth and striving toward maturity. Conversely, years in Christian experience do not remove the need for being filled with the Spirit. Indeed, experience shows some have come to the point we have reached in our studies, and still face a very basic hurdle just ahead. We turn now to this.

9

Lesson Four: My Place in the Local Church

What is the man like who has experienced all the levels of spiritual progress we have discussed thus far? Suppose he has honestly grappled with his sin tendencies and found the liberty which new truth brings. He now understands what Christ did for him and is experiencing the work of God's Spirit within his life.

Suppose further that our friend has no adequate relationship to a local church such as Scripture describes and prescribes. Ultimately, he is likely to become a frustrated person, missing God's best.

Again, he might even be a "deeper life" specialist with an extensive following. But the few who know him well will perhaps notice an independent, headstrong spirit that is not of God. Passing time leaves such a leader with limited alternatives.

1. He must maintain his position and recognition by pressing on relentlessly in his work and employing new techniques in public relations.

2. Or, he will descend quietly and unnoticed like a spent skyrocket.
3. Or, he will have to humble himself and turn to God's pattern of Christianity.

A great deal of American know-how and human ingenuity has shaped, or rather mis-shaped, the expression of Christianity as we know it today. In the minds of many people, the local church is not really at the cutting edge of the contest. Rather, multiplied numbers of Christian agencies and other efforts have taken over its responsibilities. These organizations carry on much of the evangelism and other ministries assigned by Scripture to the churches.

Without casting any reflection upon the many good people who have devised these many good works, the ones you counsel ought to be shown Jesus Christ as Head of the church—that church that is expressed in local assemblies. This is how it is in Scripture. Revelation 1 pictures the glorified Christ as presently walking among the assemblies. These make up His body on earth.

A special work of grace seems needed to lift a man's vision above the modern level of "my group doing our thing as we see it." What is required really is a new view of Jesus Christ and of the new order He came to create.

> So from now on we regard no one from a worldly point of view. Though we once regarded Christ in this way, we do so no longer. Therefore, if anyone is in Christ, he is a new creation; the old has gone, the new has come! (2 Cor. 5:16-17, (NIV).

Surely the Lord has the right to say how His bride shall equip and express herself in this world.

Careful, openhearted study needs to be made of the apostle Paul's plan as he cut into the granite of his own pagan world and shaped the body of Christ. His first action following evangelism was not to carry on an indefinite follow-up program or to establish general fellowship groups; instead, he formed local assemblies. Scripture prescribes at least some essential structure for churches. Those portions of the epistles dealing with structure are as inspired as those dealing with principles of fellowship or other doctrines.

It will be seen, then, that the term *church* as used in Scripture sometimes carries a very broad meaning:

> to him be glory in the church and in Christ Jesus throughout all generations, for ever and ever! Amen (Eph. 3:21, NIV).

On the other hand, the Bible makes abundantly clear that a church is more than a vague or arbitrary portion of the universal body of Christ. The plural term *churches* refers to assemblies of believers who gather locally. There is an element of definiteness to the term.

Notice the implication of Colossians 4:12:

> Epaphras, who is one of you and a servant of Christ Jesus, sends greetings. He is always wrestling in prayer for you, that you may stand firm in all the will of God, mature and fully assured (NIV).

Although Epaphras was away from the believers in Colosse, it was recognized that he was one of them. Accordingly, he felt deep concern for them. They were his family. He came from them and, it was to be hoped, would return to them.

There is a popular notion that wherever two or three Christians happen to be together there is a church. This is incorrect. They might properly be called a portion of the Lord's body, or family, but they are not a *church* in the technical sense. Indeed, the Scripture often used to support this incorrect idea is Matthew 18:20. A glance at verses 15-17 quickly shows that two or three do not make up a church. Rather, several believers here are instructed to carry their complaint to the church.

To help a man see his Lord more clearly, he must see the body He has left on earth as the expression of His fullness.

> *And God placed all things under his feet and appointed him to be head over everything for the church, which is his body, the fullness of him who fills everything in every way* (Eph. 1:22-23, NIV).

Many a time I have seen a Christian humble himself before these truths and experience new life. There is a definite limit as to how far and deep a believer can go without coming to terms with his own place in a local church. Apart from an exceptional calling and commissioning, which ought to be confirmed by a local assembly, one should make his primary expression of spiritual life through such a fellowship.

This is not to imply that he will be out of contact with the world. On the contrary, nothing is more relevant to the real world at every level than people, and people make up a church. When they are properly edified, they will sponsor and promote new life within each other and will encourage effective living at all levels in the outside world.

Now, all believers are by Spirit baptism brought into the body of Christ.

> For we were all baptized by one Spirit into one body—whether Jews or Greeks, slave or free—and we were all given the one Spirit to drink (1 Cor. 12:13, NIV).

Remember also that this body of our Lord expresses itself in definite local assemblies. There is power and glory in a godly family of believers having structure and a growing desire to share its life.

It is axiomatic that if no one is willing to receive spiritual ministry from another person, then no one can meaningfully give the same. Further, if no one is actively giving personal ministry, then it is not possible for others to receive it. All too often this is how the matter hangs.

Because of this absence of real caring and ministering, numbers have bolted from the traditional churches, while others use their advanced insight to cut away at churches around them. We ought to remember the patience of our Lord with the churches in Revelation 2-3. If He has not blown out the candle, let us not do it.

Some may object that a particular church is perhaps sound in doctrine but very dead in its fellowship and somewhat limited in its outreach. I do not suggest challenging a friend to the task of living joyfully among cold tombstones, but many churches lightly treated by men are loved by God. Each church deserves the opportunity to respond to a genuine ministry of individual edification.

Developing a ministry of personal edification requires no public announcement, it offers no threat to the existing leadership, it creates no flurry on the surface, nor any pocket of criticism. If individual by individual is warmed, challenged, and enlivened through deliberate edification, there should be no troubling polarization within the congregation. Instead, new life, springing up here and there from the grass roots, will bring encouragement to every worthy part of the fellowship.

Without becoming too ironclad, fellow believers should be drawn into study of the divine equipment and ministries that the Scripture sets forth in such passages as Romans 12, 1 Corinthians 12-14, Ephesians 4, and others.

A few direct questions may help friends locate satisfactory ministries in a local church. Here are some I use:

1. If you could have the one ministry you most desire, which would it be?
2. In the light of Scripture, what spiritual gift would this particular ministry require?
3. What spiritual equipment do you feel God has given you?

Next, suggest praying together over the matter for added enlightenment. Then allow the necessary time for normal growth and practice to mature these insights.

If it were not for our wily enemy, Satan, one might now go forward into all kinds of stimulating new developments. But progress is not easy, and that is precisely why we need counsel and edification from one another. Take a look now at the battle scene involving all of us.

10

Lesson Five:
The Spiritual Warfare

There is no escaping spiritual warfare. Some casualties never knew what struck them.

Even hidden defeat leaves telltale marks in a Christian's life. Such weakened believers, despite many strong points, will show themselves a bit compulsive, erratic, and driven, or will display more extreme vacillation in moods.

It might be they have taken little notice of our enemy, Satan. True enough, overconcern is destructive. But it is also true that certain teaching about Satan is necessary and helpful. Preparing even a primer on our enemy would be a large undertaking. However, the matter should receive at least some treatment in your ongoing efforts to edify others.

Approach the subject of Satan's work in a frank, unexcited, and confident manner. I will now suggest a few fundamental lessons to cover. These may be discussed and prayed over with considerable profit to those who otherwise might struggle on with shadowy questions for years.

Every growing child of God will have his periods of struggle and even suffering. Not all affliction is chastisement. Some of it comes in the course of striving to serve God against spiritual opposition.

Such passages as 1 Corinthians 15:58, Ephesians 6:10-13, and 1 Peter 5:8-10 should be looked at prayerfully.

Satan, though soundly, securely defeated, is a formidable foe when faced on the wrong ground.

The Hebrew word *Satan* indicates that he is an adversary, while the Greek term *devil* suggests that he is a diabolical slanderer. In all, he is a powerful king over legions of demons, a terror in battle, and a master deceiver. Without pity, "he never fights like a gentleman."

The vast extent of his rule boggles the mind. Scripture shows that all the millions who are yet in their sin live under his control.

> *And you were dead in your trespasses and sins, in which you formerly walked according to the course of this world, according to the prince of the power of the air* (Eph. 2:1-2, NASB).

In fact, sinners actually desire the ways of this murderer and liar.

> *You are of your father the devil, and you want to do the desires of your father. He was a murderer from the beginning, and does not stand in the truth, because there is no truth in him. Whenever he speaks a lie, he speaks from his own nature; for he is a liar, and the father of lies.* (John 8:44, NASB).

100

It will become increasingly clear as we move along this progression of thought that we are helpless against this enemy apart from an intelligent appropriation of Christ's victory made real in our experience through the ministry of the Holy Spirit.

Those who face such an enemy must either stand up and do battle intelligently and diligently or else fall in some way. We shall presently discuss how to gain and keep our liberty.

LESSON 3: BATTLING SATAN INTELLIGENTLY

Satan uses many devices against believers (2 Cor. 2:11). There will be temptations, deceptions, intimidations, hindrances, accusations, and other forms of direct and indirect attack.

LESSON 4: SATAN'S MANY DEVICES

How does Satan make these approaches to us? He may oppose us through others as the devil confronted Jesus through the disciple Peter. Or, the test might come in the form of suggestions or whisperings made more directly to the heart: "See the way they look at you? What a mess! It is all so hopeless."

Certain failure patterns give the devil a continuing advantage.

GIVING SATAN ADVANTAGE

What is Satan really trying to do? He wants more from you and me than a multiplication of failures. Scripture uncovers his larger aims. He desires to get "something" (i.e., a foothold) in you:

Hereafter I will not talk much with you: for the prince of this world cometh, and hath nothing in me (John 14:30).

He desires to gain advantage:

Lest Satan should get an advantage of us: for we are not ignorant of his devices (2 Cor. 2:11).

He desires to get some place in the life:

Neither give place to the devil (Eph. 4:27).

Jesus warned Peter:

Simon, Simon, behold, Satan hath desired to have you, that he may sift you as wheat: but I have prayed for thee, that thy faith fail not: and when thou art converted, strengthen thy brethren (Luke 22:31-32).

A list of failures that give Satan this serious, continuing advantage would include the following:

1. Habit-pattern in a particular sin, when the will is bound (see: Eph. 4:26-27).
2. Serious passivity—refusal to use ordered spiritual means of resistance and warfare.
3. Living in terms of a lie instead of the truth. Serious deception.
4. Occult involvement.

Once the devil has a close-range vantage point, he is merciless in his hounding tactics. It becomes very important to embrace the truth and refuse his deceptions.

Figure 7

God says:

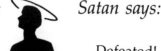

More than conqueror
(Rom. 8:37)

"I can do all things
through Christ"
(Phil. 4:13)

God is for me
(Rom. 8:31)

Satan says:

Defeated!

No good!

You can't!

Hopeless!

The important question is,
Who says so?
And, Which way are you facing?

Satan's entrenchments will continue, ever deepening, until we call a halt.

We gain our release from undue satanic pressures by (1) reestablishing ourselves in the victory of Christ and (2) exercising our spiritual weapons.

Before we take up these steps in order, let me answer a current question. What about exorcism? Never use extraordinary means when ordinary means will work. That is always a good rule to remember.

I do not say there is never a time and place for exorcism. But I may surely say that an improper exorcism, like some modern approaches to psychiatry, treats the individual as less than a per-

THIS WAY OUT

son. He is passive and not responsible while waiting for someone to do something for him. A spiritual vacuum can be dangerous.

> When an evil spirit comes out of a man, it goes through arid places seeking rest and does not find it. Then it says, "I will return to the house I left." When it arrives, it finds the house swept clean and put in order. Then it goes and takes seven other spirits more wicked than itself, and they go in and live there. And the final condition of that man is worse than the first (Luke 11:24-26, NIV).

Stay standard. Give the next needed truth to each one you counsel. Make the exception prove itself. Ordinary means will ordinarily work. Here, then, is the two-step standard procedure.

REESTABLISHING OURSELVES IN THE VICTORY OF CHRIST

We are again talking of God's provision. Satan would tease us from this sure foundation. He fastens our attention on flesh and blood, and we leave the spiritual realm where he is a defeated enemy.

Looking again at the provisions-obligations chart (p. 80) we might add that Satan is already overthrown by the cross of Jesus Christ.

> Now is the time for judgment on this world; now the prince of this world will be driven out (John 12:32, NIV).

> The reason the Son of God appeared was to destroy the devil's work (1 John 3:8, NIV).

Thus, a postscript on the chart might appear this way:

Provisions	Obligations
Satan is defeated	Resist the devil
(John 12:31; 1 John 3:8)	(James 4:7; 1 Pet. 5:8-9)

Take time for deliberately acknowledging and praising God for the coming of Christ in the flesh, His crucifixion for sin, His resurrection, and His ascension into glory. Use basic Scripture such as: John 1:14, Ephesians 1:15—2:11, and Hebrews 10.

> *For though we live in the world, we do not wage war as the world does. The weapons we fight with are not the weapons of the world. On the contrary, they have divine power to tear down strongholds. We demolish arguments and every pretension that sets itself up against the knowledge of God, and we take captive every thought to make it obedient to Christ* (2 Cor. 10:3-5, NIV).

EXERCISING OUR SPIRITUAL WEAPONS

Rehearsing and claiming again the provisions in Christ Jesus our Savior and Lord is most refreshing and spiritually revitalizing. Satan is indeed overthrown, and therefore we are enabled to fulfill the obligation to resist him.

> *Submit yourselves therefore to God. Resist the devil, and he will flee from you* (James 4:7).

There is no contradiction when we say that what Christ has done for us the Holy Spirit desires with our full cooperation to work in us. It is not surprising then to read in Scripture of both Christ's victory over Satan and that of believers who "have overcome the wicked one" (1 John

2:14). Or to be instructed that we are to resist him, "steadfast in the faith" (1 Pet. 5:9).

A proper, diligent use of truth from the Scripture and prayer in the Spirit will surely help many a Christian brother. These are our primary weapons.

To use the truth, fasten the mind definitely on a vital text that directly exalts Christ and the atonement. Incorporate it into vigorous, believing prayer. Memorize the verse if necessary. In addition to Scriptures already mentioned use Colossians 2:9-10; Hebrews 2:7-15; 1 Peter 3:22; Revelation 12:11, and others you will discover yourself.

USING "BATTLE PRAYING"   Moaning in weak prayer is not fitting here. There should be a confident embracing of truth.

Of considerable assistance to an oppressed friend would be your outlining on paper some suggestions for his guidance as he attempts to be more aggressive in prayer. Be sure you have him read the noted Scriptures as part of his prayer. Here is a sample.

1. Claim the blood offering of Jesus Christ to cover and cleanse any specific area of sin defeat.

   But if we walk in the light, as he is in the light, we have fellowship one with another, and the blood of Jesus Christ his Son cleanseth us from all sin (1 John 1:7).

2. Acknowledge Jesus Christ as Lord of all and own Him as Lord over every area of your life—especially any realm of defeat.

106

For he has rescued us from the dominion of darkness and brought us into the kingdom of the Son he loves (Col. 1:13, NIV).

3. In the name and authority of the Lord Jesus Christ resist, refuse, and order the enemy out of that area. There are times when we do not continue to plead with God about the mountain (see Mark 11:22-24). We rather speak to the mountain in the name of our Savior. Satan cannot stand on any ground presented to Jesus Christ for His rule.
4. Ask for a new filling of God's Holy Spirit.
5. Enter immediately into praise and thanksgiving for every good thing God has done for you. You may wish to use the last verses of Romans 8 in positive praise and rejoicing for all of the rich encouragement mentioned there.

As you hand the written prayer prescription to your friend, say (much as a family physician might advise), "Repeat as often as necessary." The verses and general parts of the prayer ought to be memorized for ready use in times of intense conflict.

Given proper counsel and encouragement, even those deeply ensnared may know recovery and become whole, happy persons again. There is liberty in Jesus Christ. Only let the one who assists be humble and on guard himself.

And the Lord's servant must not quarrel; instead, he must be kind to everyone, able to teach, not resentful. Those who oppose him he must gently instruct, in the hope that God will give them a change of heart leading them to a knowledge of the truth, and that they will come to their senses and escape from the trap of the devil, who has taken them captive to do his will (2 Tim. 2:24-26, NIV).

11

Lesson Six:
A Life of Intercession

I do not always include the study of prayer as a separate level of edification. At least, it would be more ideal if growth in prayer were achieved much earlier in one's progress.

Regardless, no Christian can avoid nagging dullness and burdened step if he does not come into a new prayer life.

Prayer is spiritual breathing, and someone has observed that it takes more out of you to hold your breath than to breathe. In fact, breathing adds life. You were designed to breathe. Just so, prayer should be normal. Many Christians, blue in the face, wonder why life's race is difficult.

However, we need to get far beyond self-interest in prayer and to stand for others. That is what intercession is about. Moses set the example when Israel was threatened with divine judgment.

> *Therefore He said that He*
> *would destroy them,*
> *Had not Moses His chosen one*
> *stood in the breach before*
> *Him* (Psalm 106:23, NASB).

Read Revelation 3:20 as a plea from the Lord to be allowed prayer fellowship with us:

Behold, I stand at the door, and knock: if any man hear my voice, and open the door, I will come in to him, and will sup with him, and he with me.

Does this not tug at the heart and make us hungry for this supper fellowship with Him? Truly there "are given unto us exceeding great and precious promises" (2 Pet. 1:4).

It will also come to pass that before they call, I will answer; and while they are still speaking, I will hear (Isa. 65:24, NASB).

Something that might be emphasized at every level of spiritual development should be said here: take nothing for granted. Make certain your friend understands how to pray and is practicing prayer. The repeating of old truths often brings immense benefit to a life. Never despise meat and potatoes. We eat them often.

In order to reach the depths of meaningful intercession, one must be familiar with the heights of true worship and praise. The Psalms are a great help here, of course. Train one another to make practical use of them in learning worship. Going through a Psalm, write down all the descriptions of God suggested by that text. If a description of God is actually given, jot it down. Or if a work of God is mentioned, ask, What kind of God would perform this? Then add that description to your list. When you are finished, kneel in prayer and acknowledge each item in praise to God.

Sometimes listing requests in writing before prayer is a help in stimulating alert intercession.

It will be necessary that you seek both to expand your own prayer life and also to give practical assistance to those whose prayer life is dragging. Help others get started by praying with them and checking on them here and there.

It is very invigorating for one who is weak in prayer to know that a brother is joining with him at stated times, or that you at least have agreed on certain requests that you are laboring over together. If prayer is breathing, some of the brethren need resuscitation. So do be practical.

In addition to the very large number of helpful books on prayer, I would suggest *Behind the Ranges* by Mrs. Howard Taylor (Moody Press: 1964). This includes J. O. Fraser's classic chapter on prayer, and the entire book demonstrates the power of intercession.

Does fasting help? Yes, if guarded and done in the Spirit. But an empty stomach does not guarantee a full heart. If you fast, do not become passive or complacent. Rather, actively seek the Lord's face before, during, and after the period of fasting.

According to Jesus, the most difficult cases yield *only* to serious prayer. *"And He said to them, 'This kind cannot come out by anything but prayer' "* (Mark 9:29, NASB).

THE MAIN THING: AUTHORITY

It is pathetic that often we have the right to do what we have not the strength to accomplish, and seem to have abounding strength to do what we have no right to do. But when we exercise our proper rights, God will supply strength enough.

The important thing is authority. This comes

when we position ourselves "in Him." According to John 14:13-14, to pray in the name of Jesus Christ is to have our prayers always granted.

The deep issue is that a prayer is not made in Jesus' name simply by saying, "In Jesus' name—amen." When we intelligently position ourselves on the merits of Jesus Christ, prayer will be positively answered.

Jesus teaches that our prayers will not require any last-minute begging on His part.

> *In that day you will ask in My name; and I do not say to you that I will request the Father on your behalf; for the Father Himself loves you, because you have loved Me, and have believed that I came forth from the Father* (John 16:26-27, NASB).

Notice that the success of this prayer relationship comes from our proper alignment with Jesus Christ.

As these great lessons are experienced and practiced, they will strengthen your effectiveness at every level of edification. So do not put prayer last.

12

Developing a Structured, Ongoing Plan of Edification

This book deals mainly with spontaneous individual edification. Being prepared with a seasonable word is indeed important. That is not all there is to it, however.

The purpose of this chapter is to guide you into developing your own structured plan for the regular upbuilding of another individual. The scheduled meeting together of two believers having the sole intention of being mutually edifying is a powerful, life-changing experience—especially when one of them is prepared.

Do not think of this as a course in Christian living or in individual Bible study, nor as sessions in doctrine or Christian experience. It may include much of these but only as they serve the purpose at hand.

THE AIM OF SUCH A PLAN

The immediate purpose of meeting regularly with an individual is, of course, to strengthen him where strength is most needed. The ultimate aim is to edify an edifier, to counsel a counselor. It is to provide the church of Christ with a self-starter, a kind of believer who will consciously and unconsciously revitalize others around him.

Often it is no more difficult to get a hesitating friend to agree to a series of meetings than it is to corner him for one or two sessions. The plan I have personally developed for my own ministry involves meeting for twelve or thirteen weekly sessions, an hour each.

This scheme supplies remarkable leverage to minister in almost any direction as need may require. Spiritual stalemates can be broken, marriages stirred to new freshness, sinful habits of long standing clipped at the root, and spiritual sterility brought to an end. As the individual continues through the studies, he is gradually humbled and brought to a place of readiness for new fellowship with God and man and new usefulness in the church. It is equally valuable to the new Christian and to the more experienced one. Even pastors should desire the experience and in turn see that others have the same opportunity.

Not everyone who participates with you in this plan of spiritual upbuilding will be equipped to use it regularly with others. But here and there you will find those who will be able to carry on the sessions with others, and you will have given the church a new and invaluable worker.

DEVELOPING YOUR OWN PLAN In a single chapter there is not space to give any kind of a manual of instructions. If it seems practical, perhaps the material I have used for some years can be published in a later book. However, I will outline two plans for developing

114

your own scheme of individual edification. Such a plan should not be too long, too intense, nor yet undisciplined. There has to be control and direction if you are going to realize God's best.

One plan would be to use this book as your guide. This would mean giving special attention to the steps of edification and seeking to bring your partner to each experience.

Another substantial approach, which I used in developing my own material, would place an even greater challenge before you. Make a list of the basic Christian doctrines and then list the varied duties involved in an active Christian life. Check to make certain the first list includes the Scriptures; God—Father, Son, Holy Spirit; the Person and work of Jesus Christ—His deity, human nature, earthly ministry, death, resurrection, ascension; salvation—regeneration, justification, sanctification, and growth; the church; the return of Christ; eternal destiny.

Your list of duties should detail the Christian's responsibilities in each main area of life: personal life with God, the home, the church, the world outside with its various circles. Both attitudes and actions should be reflected in your index so as to add dimension to it.

Now, if these two lists of doctrines and duties were integrated, you would have a composite, somewhat, of the entire Christian life. Would it not then be a rare and wonderful opportunity to go over all these areas with individual Christian friends? You would have the privilege of covering all the main Christian teachings, truths, or principles on the one hand and, on the other, of enlisting the proper response in each area of life. That is the direction of this particular scheme.

Of course you will want to reflect on the basic experiences God has brought into your own life and the direction in which He has been leading you. List these important life-lessons and include them in your times of instruction. Now you are prepared to develop the biblical framework. All must be taught directly from the open Bible—not from your development notes.

Choose a book of Scripture to serve as the basis for your sessions together. I recommend the gospel of John because in one way or another John touches on each doctrine and involves so many Christian duties. Read it through several times until you can determine what key texts give an opportunity to deal with the various items on your list. You will undoubtedly be amazed at the vast scope of this gospel.

If you have been sufficiently thorough, you should have a selected group of references with enough depth to enable you to bring your friends over each level of edification that I suggested in chapters 5 through 11. Keep an eye on these levels so you will have an index to the progress with your brother.

I would urge you most earnestly: avoid the inclination to give a Bible book study or to launch into an actual course in Christian living. Most people have these opportunities elsewhere in their Christian experience. Here is your chance to deal with an individual closeup, as one person to another, and your whole procedure should be determined with this in mind.

Perhaps you will have notes or outlines that you have prepared for each session. But do not use them in your fellowship meeting, as they would only hinder. Simply make a check by the verses you intend to discuss in each chapter. Be fearless in skipping as many as do not serve your immediate ends. Your fundamental objective will be to find out what your friend understands of the doctrine, or teaching, contained in each text and then to reflect with him on what response we should make to the truth found in that passage.

You will then be seeking to exercise and instruct him at three levels.

1. Comprehension—Does he really understand what the doctrine means?
2. Appropriation—Has he personally appropriated this truth as his very own?
3. Expression—Can he in turn share this in a clear, winning way with another?

I strongly urge proceeding almost altogether with questions. Question your friend when you know he does not know the answer. Question him when you already know that he knows the answer. Questioning will keep him interested and reaching forward for more and will help you to avoid talking all the time. It will be more of a sharing session, yet you will be in control and can know where you are headed.

Limit the sessions to a single brisk hour or even less. Faithfully avoid all hairsplitting and talk for talk's sake. Usually, skip the refreshments.

You will want to tell what you have learned

117

from the Word and from Christian experience. But remember, keep using questions. This way you will know how your friend looks at things, and you will be able to make your arrows strike where he really is. Be open and truly concerned for his needs. With definite purpose of heart, see him through to higher ground.

AN EXAMPLE To clarify, permit me to illustrate a portion of one of these guided fellowship sessions. You and your friend are sitting together at the kitchen table, in the den, or in the study—each with open Bible. After prayer you are discussing selected verses in John. Suppose your next stop is John 5:39, and you have him read it aloud.

> *You search the Scriptures, because you think that in them you have eternal life; and it is these that bear witness of Me* (NASB).

You ask, "According to this verse, what is the focal point of all the Scriptures?" Next you might add a comment or two about 2 Timothy 3:16-17.

You continue, "According to John 5:39, when we neglect to read our Bibles, we are shutting off God's vital Word of testimony to us concerning His Son. At present, where are you reading in the Bible daily?"

My experience indicates that most believers are not in a regular practice of Bible reading. A polite and disarming question such as I have suggested usually makes an individual open to your proposing a plan of daily study through Scripture. Sealing this with prayer together—confessing failure and dedicating yourselves to new effort—will be a great help.

Procede in a similar vein with other areas of doctrine and duty.

As you near the end of your prescribed fellowship times, prayerfully face the question: Could this partner now possibly do this with a friend of his? God will help you make this judgment.

Announcing this goal at the outset is ruinous to the whole concept of personal discipleship. Things will tend to deteriorate to a level where you are simply telling him things so he can in turn give them to others. Such an ill-advised approach will surely short-circuit the powerful truths so they will not touch his heart.

Perhaps you will soon be led to one who does have promise as an instructor of others. Encourage him to bring to your final session the name of a friend with whom he might be willing to share these studies. If his choice seems good, encourage him or even help him to make a contact and get started.

It is usually unwise to confront a prospective partner with the idea of a long series of meetings or a specialized course. Simply give him the idea that meeting together as friends could be mutually profitable, and that you yourself have already found it so. An approach that generally works well is to invite the prospect to your home for coffee. Then get out the Bibles and have a brief study tending toward the kind of question and answer fellowship that would later characterize the regular studies. If the meeting appears beneficial, ask him if he would like to do this again, and propose a time and place.

119

Since only two individuals are involved, you will find great flexibility in moving the meeting time when there is conflict. But do not skip a week unless it is absolutely necessary.

In a short while you will notice changes begin to take place in your friend's life and possibly in your own. This ought to spread to others in the church. However, the ministry will prosper most if kept private and unannounced.

Make certain the pastor or other responsible leaders understand what you are doing. Indicate to them that you are not working toward any group meeting, nor will the meetings with any individual continue indefinitely. (And, by the way, remember this is a very good rule. Do not go on and on. Keep your natural desires well-pruned.)

Always, I would urge one to begin in his own home with his spouse. This can be difficult, but it is fine for humbling! (Later, take each of your children individually.) After all, your partner is next to you in the body of Christ. This is where true church life begins. Afterward, you and your husband or wife can take on other couples, but never make the studies a foursome. Using separate rooms, always meet one with one. Or, have the wives get together at a different time than the men.

After the initial friendly contact, these sharing times can be carried on in a serious way without taking the entire morning or evening. One hour is enough, if agreed on in advance. May the Head of the church lead many into the high and serious endeavor of building up His body.

For God did not give us a spirit of timidity, but a spirit of power, of love and of self-discipline (2 Tim. 1:7, NIV).

By now it should be clear that anyone who takes up this ministry of individual edification must himself be right with God. The secretly fallen man may continue to function publicly, but he will soon shrink from meaningful, private, face to face encounters with a brother. However, after one's own showdown with God, the eyes see more clearly the major areas of Christian life. It is normal to share with others, and in sharing we ourselves are blessed. And remember:

If one member suffers, all the members suffer with it; if one member is honored, all the members rejoice with it (1 Cor. 12:26, NASB).

May our Lord, who touched the lepers and reached for His sinking disciple Peter, give us ears to hear their cry "Save me!" The cry may be inaudible—even intentionally muted by sophisticated deception—but, underneath, many want something better. You can give it to them and share their joy as the long night is ended.

> *Counselors of peace have*
> *joy.*
> *Those who deal faithfully*
> *are His delight*
> (Prov. 12:20*b*, 22*b*, NASB).

Notes

Notes

Notes

Notes

Notes